Royal Liverpool
Golf Club

135TH OPEN CHAMPIONSHIP
Card of the Championship Course

Hole	Par	Yards	Hole	Par	Yards
1	4	454	10	5	534
2	4	436	11	4	393
3	4	429	12	4	448
4	4	372	13	3	198
5	5	528	14	4	456
6	3	202	15	3	161
7	4	453	16	5	554
8	4	423	17	4	459
9	3	198	18	5	560
Out	35	3,495	In	37	3,763
			Total	72	7,258

C000145511

Aurum Press
25 Bedford Avenue, London WC1B 3AT

Published 2006 by Aurum Press

Copyright © 2006 R&A Championships Limited

Statistics of The 135th Open Championship produced on a
Unisys Computer System

Course map courtesy of The Majors of Golf

"Back To Where It Once Belonged" (page 17) was inspired by an article of the same title
by Eric Levin in *Travel and Leisure Golf* magazine.

Assistance with records provided by Peter Lewis,
Stewart McDougall and Salvatore Johnson

A CIP catalogue record for this book is available
from the British Library

ISBN-10: 1 84513 202 5
ISBN-13: 978 1 84513 202 6

All rights reserved. No part of this publication may be reproduced,
stored in a retrieval system, or transmitted in any form or by any means,
electronic, mechanical, photocopying, recording, or otherwise,
without the prior permission of the publishers.

Design and production by IMG Creative & Davis Design
Printed in Great Britain by Butler & Tanner Ltd

THE OPEN CHAMPIONSHIP

WRITERS
Andy Farrell
Mike Aitken
David Davies
John Hopkins
Lewine Mair
Michael McDonnell

PHOTOGRAPHERS
Getty Images

David Cannon
Stuart Franklin
Ross Kinnaird
Warren Little
Andy Lyons
Andrew Redington

Scott Halleran
Rob Harborne
Richard Martin-Roberts
Golf Editors
Steve Rose
Chief Editor

EDITOR
Bev Norwood

The Championship Committee

CHAIRMAN
Martin Kippax

DEPUTY CHAIRMAN
Geoffrey Clay

COMMITTEE

Gavin Caldwell	George MacGregor
John Crawshaw	Jim McArthur
Charles Donald	Lout Mangelaar Meertens
Alan Holmes	Jeremy Monroe
Rodney James	Nigel Watt

ADVISORY MEMBER
Desmond Duffy
Council of National Golf Unions

CHIEF EXECUTIVE
Peter Dawson

DIRECTOR OF CHAMPIONSHIPS
David Hill

DIRECTOR OF RULES AND EQUIPMENT STANDARDS
David Rickman

The R&A is golf's world rules and development body and organiser of The Open Championship. It operates with the consent of more than 125 national and international, amateur and professional organisations, from over 110 countries and on behalf of an estimated 28 million golfers in Europe, Africa, Asia-Pacific and The Americas (outside the USA and Mexico). The United States Golf Association (USGA) is the game's governing body in the United States and Mexico.

Introduction

By Martin Kippax
Chairman of Championship Committee
The R&A

The year 2006 saw the return of The 135th Open Championship to Royal Liverpool Golf Club at Hoylake after an absence of 39 years. From every perspective, this year's Championship proved to be a great success. A hot, dry summer leading up to The Open ensured true links conditions, with a fast running course and hardly a green blade of grass in sight on the fairways. The course was in perfect order and the wonderful weather enabled Craig Gilholm and his team to present the course in superb condition. This was fully appreciated by the players and acknowledged by them in their interviews and generous comments throughout Open week.

After such a lengthy absence there were, unsurprisingly, doubters who believed the course was not up to the task of providing a satisfactory Open venue. They could not have been more wrong. The enthusiasm and effort shown by the Royal Liverpool members and their Championship Committee would be hard to surpass. The crowds were friendly, knowledgeable and turned up in their tens of thousands to provide a record for an Open Championship held in England. Over 230,000 enthusiasts witnessed some spectacular golf by the finest of players, which resulted in a most exciting leaderboard on Saturday evening.

On Sunday the acknowledged world number one spun his own inimitable magic and Tiger Woods emerged the winner. A more clinical and professional round of golf would be hard to imagine.

I must thank the Hoylake Championship Committee and the many hundreds of volunteers for their enthusiastic assistance in running all of our qualifying events and The Open Championship itself.

Martin Kippax

Foreword

By Tiger Woods

There has never been a championship in which I experienced so many different emotions as I did during The Open at Royal Liverpool. In the end, I was both excited and worn out.

Never did I think any Open victory would mean more to me than my two at St Andrews, but this one does. To win for the first time after my father passed away, and for that to be a major championship, makes this very special. My feelings came pouring out at the end, when I thought of what my father meant to me and I wished that he could have seen me win one more. He would have been very proud, because he always told me to think my way around a golf course and not let my emotions get the better of me. He was adamant that I should play that way, and this week I did.

I had amazing support from my wife, Elin, and from Steve Williams, Hank Haney, Keith Kelvin, Mark Steinberg, and everyone around us. For the first time, my mother was not here for The Open. She was at home watching on television, and it was fun to go back and share this with her.

My game was close to where I needed to have it when I arrived, and in my practice rounds everything got better each day. I felt a conservative approach was the way to go. I realised early on that I would not be using my driver much, if at all. The ball was going 350 to 370 yards and there was no way to control that. I felt if I stayed out of bunkers and putted reasonably well, I would be in contention to the end. I hit the ball well all week and, except for the last nine holes on Saturday, I had a really good touch on the greens. My strategy was sound and it kept me out of trouble.

It was never easy because several of the others, and Chris DiMarco, in particular, played beautiful golf and kept the pressure on me.

This is a victory I will treasure.

Tiger Woods

The Venue

A Rigorous Form Of Golf

By Michael McDonnell

History has shown at Royal Liverpool that the champion must be capable of more than hitting great shots. He must be able to play through adversity.

The paradox of the Royal Liverpool Golf Club on the shores of the Dee Estuary is that it holds an imperishable place in the history of golf and is acknowledged to be one of the most demanding championship tests, yet it had remained virtually unknown and uncharted territory for almost 40 years until 2006 to the world's greatest golfers.

The true measure of its challenge, which extends over the links close to the village of Hoylake, was best defined by the venerable Bernard Darwin, who observed: "Hoylake golf is never, as it seems to me, slack or casual. It is the golf of men rigorously brought up who will always do their best and die if need be in the last of their own sacred ditches."

Dunes fortify the par-3 No 13 (left), while the par-4 No 17 (preceding pages) requires two well-placed shots to reach the green.

Permissible hyperbole perhaps, but Darwin made his point about the special demands of this open and largely unprotected terrain, and indeed his successor on *The Times*, Peter Ryde, came to much the same conclusion when he wrote: "Opens at Royal Liverpool are won by courage more than brilliance and this is due to the nature of the links which demands the first quality to a marked degree and in some ways seems to subdue the second."

Indeed there have been countless illustrations in the 10 previous Opens played over the links of Hoylake to demonstrate that most important ingredient to success, none more so than when Bobby Jones captured the 1930 title, which formed the second leg of what was to be his Grand Slam performance of winning Open and Amateur titles on both sides of the Atlantic in the same year.

In the final round Jones suddenly ran up a 7 at the eighth hole after hitting two faultless strokes to the edge of the green then squandering another five to hole out. He said later: "It is the most inexcusable hole I have ever played. An old man with a croquet mallet could have got down in two. I will play that hole over a thousand times in my dreams."

The green on the par-4 No 3 hole is relatively flat, but there is a hollow to the left.

But the significant fact that supports the Darwin and Ryde theory is that Jones put the nightmare behind him, focused on the job in hand, and went on to earn the silver Claret Jug before returning home to capture the other titles and then retiring from the competitive game. Jones was not the only one to make a piece of history that day. His chronicler, the Atlanta journalist O B Keeler, described his victory on radio across the Atlantic, the first time an overseas sporting event had been broadcast to an American audience.

Another, more recent example of the kind of play required to win The Open occurred in the 1967 Championship, the last time the event was played at Hoylake. Robert de Vicenzo, the courtly Argentinean professional who suspected as he reached the age of 44 that he was coming to the end of a career in which numerous winning chances had passed him by, suddenly found himself with another golden chance as he led in the final round.

Only Jack Nicklaus posed a major threat and the obvious question was whether the hitherto fickle temperament of de Vicenzo could hold out over one of the most brutal finishing stretches in championship golf. On the 16th hole (this year being used as the 18th because it was thought to be a better closing hole), Roberto drove perilously close to the practice ground, which flanked the right side of the fairway and was out of bounds.

Herewith an eyewitness account of the moment: "Roberto now faced the dilemma of whether to hit across the vast stretch of out-of-bounds territory to reach the green on the other side or play safe and strengthen Big Jack's chances. Boldly, he reached for his spoon and swung gently but purposefully at the ball, which rose clear of the bank in front of him and soared towards the green. The crisis had passed and Roberto strode to victory."

Walter Hagen faced his own personal crisis in the last round of The Open in 1924 when he lurched over the outward nine holes in 41 strokes and knew he had to play par golf on the homeward stretch to stand any chance of success. He struggled on to the then 15th hole into the teeth of a wind and realised the green was not reachable with his second shot unless he took a driver from the fairway. It was a new club in his bag and he was not totally confident about its performance. Even so, The Haig knew he had no choice but to swing it. The ensuing shot held the ball so low it never rose more than 15 feet and rolled onto the green.

Royal Liverpool has been widely acknowledged as part of the fabric of golf and a place from which innovations and ideas have flowed constantly down the years. At the end of the 19th century the club had its own set of rules for the game that, for a time, found growing popularity among other clubs until the common code from St Andrews was adopted.

It initiated the Amateur Championship as well as the English Amateur Championship. It was the venue for an impromptu match between amateurs from the United States—Bobby Jones and Francis Ouimet played—and a British team that was the forerunner to the Walker Cup. Hoylake was also the place where the gutta-percha ball met its demise when Sandy Herd won The Open in 1902 with the rubber-cored Haskell ball and set the style others had to follow.

Moreover, it was the home club to two of the greatest amateur golfers of their day, John Ball and Harold Hilton, who between them won three Opens and 12 Amateur titles. They are the only amateurs other than Jones ever to have won The Open Championship. Ball won the Amateur eight times, was the first amateur golfer and Englishman to win The Open and, though he shunned the limelight, was undoubtedly the local hero.

Henry Leach, one the leading golf writers of the day, observed: "He is one of the most modest men alive. He has never written an article about his achievements, has never been interviewed, and he is not available to the general public. When he has finished his game he just shuts himself up to all but his friends."

After one triumph, Ball got off the train at the stop before Hoylake and walked home along the sands because he knew fans would be waiting at the station to greet him. Horace Hutchinson described his swing as "such a beautiful exhibition of grace and power, showing such ability in a moment and on a spot." Asked to describe his success in one championship, Ball explained: "I was hitting my drives the right height for the day."

Hilton was more flamboyant and outgoing. He won The Open in

In the Words of the Competitors...

"

"It's certainly not a place you want to come to play for the first time. You need to have an idea of how to play on this golf course."
—Jim Furyk

"Any tee you can hit three or four different clubs off the tee, if the wind changes even the slightest bit."
—Padraig Harrington

"Overall it's going to be a fantastic challenge this week to play a golf course this fast. We don't get a chance very often, but when we do, it sure brings shot-making and creativity back into the game."
—Tiger Woods

"It's going to be really pure links golf this week."
—Ernie Els

"The more I've played here, I've really appreciated how well the course was designed."
—Phil Mickelson

"The course is playing very short right now, which makes it tricky because you're running through into bunkers and into rough."
—Luke Donald

1892 when the Championship was first extended to four rounds and then again in 1897. He captured the Amateur title four times and preceded Bobby Jones in 1911 by holding both the British and US Amateur titles at the same time. He wrote books about his experiences and later served as editor of a golf magazine.

His sturdy character and personality are probably best defined by an account of an Amateur Championship final in front a partisan Scottish crowd at St Andrews "cheering on their own hero whose good shots were applauded to the echo but those played by Mr Hilton were watched in oppressive silence, his mistakes being hailed with every sign of jubilation. He ignored the expressions of partisanship, summoned up all his pluck, resourcefulness and cheerful philosophy and achieved a brilliant triumph."

Such dominant figures amongst its membership simply added to a widespread recognition that Royal Liverpool was one of the most important clubs in golf. It was established in 1869 on part of a very popular racecourse and shared its activity with the sport of kings for seven years until the racing stopped, perhaps because golfers were irritated at having to play out of hoof marks (no free drop in those days). Some mementos of those racing days prevail. Two holes are named Stand and Course and the saddling bell is now used to summon members to dinner in the clubhouse.

Royal Liverpool has been the scene of many historic moments. Arnaud Massy became the first Frenchman to win The Open when he triumphed in 1907, and the list of victors also includes J H Taylor (1913), Alf Padgham (1936), Fred Daly (1947), and Peter Thomson (1956). The Irishman Daly's triumph was also a moment of heartbreak for American challenger Frank Stranahan who, needing an eagle 2 on the final hole to force a playoff, left his second shot inches from the hole.

Sir Michael Bonallack won the 1969 Amateur Championship here when he beat Bill Hyndman, and the great Irish golfer Joe Carr defeated E. Harvie Ward for the title in 1953. Richard Davies won the

Royal Liverpool Golf Club had been host to 10 previous Open Championships and has a rich history.

Round Royal Liverpool

No 1 • 454 yards Par 4
The drive must favour the left side, avoiding three bunkers hidden from the tee. The green has been relocated away from the road, but the threat of out of bounds is ever present.

No 2 • 436 yards Par 4
A new back tee increases this hole by 19 yards, adding to the demands of an accurate tee shot between two sets of bunkers for a second shot to a deep green surrounded by more bunkers.

No 3 • 429 yards Par 4
The tee shot should land as near as possible to the corner of the dogleg. There is out of bounds flanking the right all the way to the flat green, which has a hollow to the left.

No 4 • 372 yards Par 4
There is a slight right-hand dogleg so that the tee shot should favour the left side of the fairway to open up the green, which has been moved back and is surrounded by bunkers and is as difficult to hold as its predecessor because of its slopes.

No 5 • 528 yards Par 5
A left-hand dogleg requires a pinpoint drive between two sets of bunkers to face the prospect of a long second shot to a green that has been pushed back 40 yards and heavily protected with bunkers.

No 6 • 202 yards Par 3
The first of Hoylake's exhaustive short holes requires an iron to a pedestal green surrounded by deep bunkers. The tee has been adjusted to provide a more demanding angle of attack, but there is the slight compensation that a shot that hits the bank on the right invariably bounces back to the putting surface.

No 7 • 453 yards Par 4
The tee shot should favour the right side of the fairway, but that still leaves a difficult second shot away from the two left-hand bunkers at the front of the green which tend to gather the ball that is not steered safely clear.

No 8 • 423 yards Par 4
The drive must be hit bravely over the marker post, but a ball too far to the left could leave the player with a blind second shot to an otherwise large and accommodating green.

No 9 • 198 yards Par 3
An intimidating prospect. Changes to this hole included an elevated tee, a re-contoured approach, and new sandhills that eased some of the fear, but the demand to hit the green or face dire consequences remains the same.

No 10 • 534 yards Par 5
The drive should find the right half of the fairway, leaving a long second shot up the slight hill leading to the green, which falls sharply away to left and right, so that those who do not get home in two still have a testing chip shot.

No 11 • 393 yards Par 4
This is the start of the stretch along the Dee Estuary. Even a straight drive finds a slight bowl in the fairway, prompting a blind second shot to a green that is angled left to right.

No 12 • 448 yards Par 4
A new tee has added 35 yards to this hole, but the challenge remains the same. The tee shot must be played to the left side of the fairway, which slopes towards the right. Three bunkers set in the sandhills are positioned to snare the sliced shot. The second shot is played to a raised green protected by grassy hollows.

No 13 • 198 yards Par 3
The tee shot that does not make the distance will be heavily punished, because this green is fortified by dunes and more crucially by a bunker that offers obvious menace to the tentative shot that is even slightly short.

No 14 • 456 yards Par 4
There is a left-hand dogleg which poses a threat to long hitters who attempt to cut the corner because a new position for the bunkers threatens the carry which still leaves a second shot over the right edge of a hill to a fairly narrow green.

No 15 • 161 yards Par 3
This is the shortest, but still one of the trickiest, of the short holes that requires a brave and extremely accurate tee shot to a narrow green that is surrounded by a chain of cavernous bunkers.

No 16 • 554 yards Par 5
The tee shot must favour the right side of the fairway to allow a fairly safe run to the green, avoiding two new large bunkers en route. The green itself is more tightly bunkered and has a grassy hollow on the right.

No 17 • 459 yards Par 4
Here is a case of "what you see is what you get." It is an honest hole with no hidden perils, but it still requires two well-placed shots to find the green.

No 18 • 560 yards Par 5
The drive must be taken as close as possible to the edge of the right-hand dogleg, but not risking the out of bounds which could come into play on the second shot. This hole presents a birdie chance, but not worth the possibility of disaster.

1962 Championship, Vinny Giles beat Mark James for the 1975 Championship, and Gordon Sherry won in 1995. Jay Sigel led the US Walker Cup squad to victory at Hoylake in 1983.

Women's golf also has been strongly represented at Hoylake, and the British and Irish squad won the 1992 Curtis Cup here. Helen Dobson took the 1989 British Women's title, and Kelli Kuehne won the 1996 trophy in a double triumph as she became the first American player to hold both the British and US titles in the same year.

It was a long overdue tit-for-tat response, because in 1913 Gladys Ravenscroft, already British champion, lifted the American title. She went on to become the first captain of Royal Liverpool Ladies Golf Club and unwittingly advanced the cause of women's liberation during the 1909 Ladies Championship at Royal Birkdale, on a very hot summer's day, when she shocked Edwardian society by rolling up her sleeves to expose her bare arms!

And so, to the obvious question. Why had Royal Liverpool been removed from The Open Championship map for almost 40 years? Or rather, how has it come back? The answer is that, at long last, it has been able to combine its inarguable playing merits with the essential infrastructure of a major sporting contest that has grown to global proportions in the 21st century.

The green on the par-4 No 2 hole is surrounded by bunkers.

Back To Where It Once Belonged

By Lewine Mair

They say it is no coincidence that the fortunes of Liverpool and the Royal Liverpool Golf Club at Hoylake have mirrored each other over the last 136 years. When, in 1869, George Morris, the brother of Old Tom, came from St Andrews to lay out nine holes for the would-be members, England's second port was at once fashionable and bustling. Samuel Cunard had established the first shipping line carrying passengers from Liverpool to North America in 1840, while trading connections had brought an eclectic mix of races from all corners of the world.

Among a host of handsome buildings, Liverpool University and the Picton Library were up and running in the 1880s, with the following verse on the Picton capturing much of the atmosphere among the early gentlemen golfers at Hoylake.

*"You can't make a noise in
the Picton,
They won't stand a clatter
or brawl,
You must ask for your books
With intelligent looks
Or you won't get a volume
at all."*
—Maud Budden

Other architectural landmarks of those days included the 18th century Town Hall, the 19th century St George's Hall, and the neo-Gothic Anglican Cathedral which was founded in 1904 but not completed until 1978. The Roman Catholic Metropolitan Cathedral would be started and finished in the mid-1960s, with the strikingly modern architecture long denoting rather more of a song and dance than the Beatles themselves.

The cathedral opened its doors in 1967, the same year that Roberto de Vicenzo withstood a late charge by Jack Nicklaus to win the last Open at Hoylake. A measure of its importance, at that time the only venue that had hosted more Opens than Royal Liverpool (10) was St Andrews (12).

That was also the era in its history that Liverpool produced the musical group that rocked the world. The Beatles had a tremendous effect on Liverpool's reputation and self-image. Suburbanites suddenly were part of Liverpool, but Liverpudlians did not always return the favour, though John Lennon's first wife, Cynthia, was from Hoylake.

It was in the summer of 1967 that the Beatles released *Sgt. Pepper's Lonely Hearts Club Band*. There were three sportsmen among the diverse celebrities on the cover—Johnny Weissmuller, Sonny Liston, and Albert Stubbins of English football fame. But there were none of the golfing heroes of the day. The Beatles may have featured in a famous photo-shoot at Liverpool's Allerton Municipal Golf Club, but they were never

The Beatles Story attracts tourists to Liverpool.

among those musicians to be caught up in golf's swing.

Though the Cavern Club, where the Beatles had started, was siring new talent all the time and events of 1967 smacked of a city in the ascendancy, the truth was that it had hit rock bottom. Probably more than anywhere else in Britain, it was in the throes of a financial slump. With England having joined the Common Market, the Atlantic port was no longer seen as a centre of the universe even by its citizens. There were strikes and skirmishes as people were laid off. Something had to be done.

The docks were an obvious starting point and Albert Dock was tackled first. Today, it houses shops, restaurants, and three Museums, one of which is devoted to The Beatles Story.

When Lennon was murdered in 1980, pilgrims began to flock to his hometown and, very soon, there were Beatles tours to haunts known wherever the group's songs have been sung—Penny Lane and Strawberry Fields to name but two.

These days workers on construction cranes and crews are labouring eight days a week to bring about a new Liverpool, including the nearly £1 billion Paradise Project which will feature about 40 new buildings including hotels, residences, and fashionable shops.

For Royal Liverpool, the first hint that The Open would return to their strip of linksland came in 1995 when the club, known as the home of the Amateur Championship, housed what was its 17th Amateur. Having heard rumours that the powers-that-be deemed their club too small for the demands of a modern Open, they purchased more land and dispatched a series of aerial photographs to The R&A.

The R&A agreed that the links could return to The Open rota, but it was on the proviso that certain adjustments were made not just to the course but to local traffic patterns. Hoylake Municipal, over the road, helped The Open cause when they threw in their lot with their distinguished neighbours, happily agreeing to their £10-a-round course being used as a practice ground and a car park for the week.

The members of the Royal Liverpool Golf Club are suitably grateful for the alliance, recognising full well that The Open belongs to the area as much as to them. They are part of the rich tapestry of the modern Liverpool scene and they are proud to belong.

To the chagrin of the women members, the club's dinners remain all-male affairs. Yet, when it comes to the dinner dances that nowadays punctuate the calendar, it is said that even the oldest member will jump to his feet at the first bar of the Beatles.

It's Now Truly The World's Open

73 percent of the players come from 21 overseas countries, including 43 Americans

By Bev Norwood

In the 39 years between visits to Hoylake, The Open Championship had grown into something much more international than it had been in 1967. Of those playing that year at Royal Liverpool Golf Club, 91 were from Great Britain and Ireland and 39 were from the rest of the world. British and Irish players represented 70 percent of the 130-man field. This year that figure had fallen to 27 percent, as there were 42 British and Irish players and 114 overseas players in the field of 156 men.

Between 1967 and 2006 the biggest difference was the number of players from the United States. There were just seven Americans in 1967—and one of those was an amateur—and this year there were 43 Americans, one more than the British and Irish group.

Roberto de Vicenzo, the champion in 1967, was from Argentina, one of 10 countries that provided one player each. Australia and South Africa had nine players each, and four came from Italy. This year players came from 21 overseas countries, including 23 from Australia, 10 from South Africa, and 6 each from Spain, Sweden, and Japan. The Open had not necessarily become more cosmopolitan over that time. After all, three came from Egypt in 1968, none this year.

The American entry in 1967 consisted of Jack Nicklaus, who was second by two strokes, Deane Beman, the 1959 Amateur champion, Doug Sanders, Phil Rodgers, Bert Yancey, Gay Brewer, and the amateur Bob Sweeny, the only one of the group who missed the 36-hole cut.

Arnold Palmer has been widely credited with breathing new life into The Open with his appearances starting in the early 1960s, when he came to St Andrews in 1960, placed second, then returned to win in 1961 at Royal Birkdale and in 1962 at Troon.

The idea of the modern Grand Slam—consisting of the Masters, US Open, The Open Championship, and US-PGA Championship—that Palmer created in 1960 had not really caught on yet. That was the professional version of the original Grand Slam of Bobby Jones in 1930, which was the Amateur and Open championships of Great Britain and the United States.

Palmer stayed home in 1967 to better prepare for the USPGA, which he had never won (and never would), starting five days after The Open, in Denver, almost 7,000 miles apart. It did not do Palmer much good. He tied for 14th place, six strokes behind. Of the six US professionals at Hoylake, all but Beman rushed back to compete in the USPGA, and all survived the 36-hole cut (Yancey then withdrew). Nicklaus tied for third place, missing by one stroke the playoff won by Don January over Don Massengale.

For five years in the 1960s, The Open and USPGA were played on back-to-back weeks and before that, in 1951 and 1953, the championships overlapped. In his annual book, *The World of Professional Golf* for 1967, Mark McCormack, then the business manager for Palmer, Nicklaus, and many others, wrote that he was worried about the impact of the USPGA on The Open as a great international event. That fear was not realised, and after 1968 the dates for the USPGA were moved away.

McCormack was probably correct in his view that the USPGA looked upon The Open warily, and did so for years before accepting a coexistence, even after the touring players broke away from the PGA of America and formed the PGA Tour. By the mid-1970s, Beman had become the PGA Tour commissioner and offered a proposal that releases should be required for his players to compete in The Open. The idea never took off.

The reason for Beman's concern was the growing number of PGA Tour members who were in The Open and were missing from his tournaments for one or more weeks in the heart of the summer.

By 1970 at St Andrews, the number of overseas players had grown to 55,

Roberto de Vicenzo was the first Argentinean champion.

including 24 Americans, and in 1977 at Turnberry—just 10 years after The Open at Royal Liverpool—there were 73 overseas players, 26 from the United States. That was the year of the great duel between Nicklaus and Tom Watson, and the Americans rolled over the rest of the field, taking 11 of the top 12 places. Only Tommy Horton, who tied for ninth, broke the American sequence.

At that time The Open was just beginning to attract the average players on the PGA Tour. It was an expensive trip from America, the prize money had not yet reached astronomical figures, and The Open then was often perceived in the United States as an event for proven champions like Palmer and Nicklaus, and others who would dare challenge them. American players who had yet to contend in major championships or other significant events might not have entered in those days.

Times have changed. For the convenience of players worldwide, International Final Qualifying events for The Open are now held in Asia, Australasia, Africa, and the United States, in addition to Europe. Reaching back to embrace The Open, the Americans have stretched all the way to Young Tom Morris, who is now listed in the PGA Tour Media Guide, sharing the record for "most consecutive victories in a single event" with Walter Hagen, Gene Sarazen, and Tiger Woods.

Exempt Competitors

Name, Country	Category
Robert Allenby, Australia	3
Stephen Ames, Canada	3, 12
Billy Andrade, USA	15
Stuart Appleby, Australia	3, 17
Severiano Ballesteros, Spain	2
Rich Beem, USA	11
John Bickerton, England	7
Thomas Bjorn, Denmark	3, 4
Paul Broadhurst, England	6
Bart Bryant, USA	3, 13
Angel Cabrera, Argentina	3, 4, 5, 17
Mark Calcavecchia, USA	2, 21
Chad Campbell, USA	3, 13
Michael Campbell, New Zealand	1, 3, 4, 9, 17
Paul Casey, England	3, 6
K J Choi, South Korea	3
Stewart Cink, USA	3, 17
Tim Clark, South Africa	3, 17
Darren Clarke, Northern Ireland	3, 4
Fred Couples, USA	1, 3, 17
Ben Crane, USA	3, 13
Ben Curtis, USA	2
John Daly, USA	2
Chris DiMarco, USA	3, 13, 17
Stephen Dodd, Wales	4
Luke Donald, England	3, 4, 13
Nick Dougherty, England	4
Bradley Dredge, Wales	4
Scott Drummond, Scotland	5
David Duval, USA	2
Johan Edfors, Sweden	6
Ernie Els, South Africa	2, 3, 4
Nick Faldo, England	2
Niclas Fasth, Sweden	4
Gonzalo Fernandez-Castano, Spain	3
Kenneth Ferrie, England	4
Marcus Fraser, Australia	8
Keiichiro Fukabori, Japan	23
Fred Funk, USA	12, 13, 17
Jim Furyk, USA	3, 9, 13, 17

Name, Country	Category
Sergio Garcia, Spain	1, 3, 4, 13
Lucas Glover, USA	3
Mathew Goggin, Australia	16
Retief Goosen, South Africa	1, 3, 4
*Julien Guerrier, France	27
Todd Hamilton, USA	2
Padraig Harrington, Republic of Ireland	3, 13
J J Henry, USA	15
Mark Hensby, Australia	17
Tim Herron, USA	3
S K Ho, South Korea	24
David Howell, England	3, 4, 5
Tatsuhiko Ichihara, Japan	24
Yasuharu Imano, Japan	23
Miguel Angel Jimenez, Spain	3, 4
Brandt Jobe, USA	3
Zach Johnson, USA	3
Robert Karlsson, Sweden	7
Shingo Katayama, Japan	3, 22
Simon Khan, England	3
Bernhard Langer, Germany	1
Paul Lawrie, Scotland	2
Tom Lehman, USA	2, 3
Peter Lonard, Australia	17
Davis Love III, USA	3, 13, 17
Sandy Lyle, Scotland	2
Hunter Mahan, USA	16
Paul McGinley, Republic of Ireland	3, 4
Shaun Micheel, USA	11
Phil Mickelson, USA	3, 10, 11, 13, 17
*Edoardo Molinari, Italy	28
Colin Montgomerie, Scotland	1, 3, 4
Toshinori Muto, Japan	25
Arron Oberholser, USA	3, 14
Geoff Ogilvy, Australia	1, 3, 9
Sean O'Hair, USA	13
Nick O'Hern, Australia	3, 17, 19
Jose Maria Olazabal, Spain	1, 3
Mark O'Meara, USA	2
Rod Pampling, Australia	3, 14

Name, Country	Category	Name, Country	Category
Kenny Perry, USA	3, 13, 17	David Smail, New Zealand	24
Wayne Perske, Australia	24	Henrik Stenson, Sweden	3, 4
Carl Pettersson, Sweden	3	Hideto Tanihara, Japan	25
Ian Poulter, England	4	*Marius Thorp, Norway	29
Andres Romero, Argentina	8	Scott Verplank, USA	3, 13, 17
Rory Sabbatini, South Africa	3, 14	Anthony Wall, England	8
Charl Schwartzel, South Africa	20	Tom Watson, USA	2, 26
Adam Scott, Australia	3, 12, 13, 17, 19	Mike Weir, Canada	3, 10, 17
John Senden, Australia	16	Thaworn Wiratchant, Thailand	18
Vijay Singh, Fiji	1, 3, 11, 13, 17	Tiger Woods, USA	1, 2, 3, 9, 10, 13, 17
Jeff Sluman, USA	3		

*Denotes amateurs

Key to Exemptions from Regional, Local Final and International Final Qualifying

Exemptions for 2006 were granted to the following:

(1) First 10 and anyone tying for 10th place in the 2005 Open Championship at St Andrews.

(2) Past Open Champions aged 65 or under on 23 July 2006.

(3) The first 50 players on the Official World Golf Ranking for Week 22, 2006.

(4) First 20 in the PGA European Tour Final Order of Merit for 2005.

(5) The BMW Championship winners for 2004-2006.

(6) First 3 and anyone tying for 3rd place, not exempt, in the top 20 of the PGA European Tour Order of Merit for 2006 on completion of the 2006 BMW Championship.

(7) First 2 European Tour members and any European Tour members tying for 2nd place, not exempt, in a cumulative money list taken from all official PGA European Tour events from the British Masters up to and including the Open de France and including The US Open.

(8) The leading player, not exempt, in the first 10 and ties of each of the 2006 Open de France, 2006 Smurfit European Open and the 2006 Barclays Scottish Open. Ties will be decided by the better final round score and, if still tied, by the better third round score and then by the better second round score. If still tied, a hole by hole card playoff will take place starting at the 18th hole of the final round.

(9) The US Open Champions for 2002-2006.

(10) The US Masters Champions for 2002-2006.

(11) The USPGA Champions for 2001-2005.

(12) The USPGA Tour Players Champions for 2004-2006.

(13) First 20 on the Official Money List of the USPGA Tour for 2005.

(14) First 3 and anyone tying for 3rd place, not exempt, in the top 20 of the Official Money List of the USPGA Tour for 2006 on completion of the FedEx St Jude Classic.

(15) First 2 USPGA Tour members and any USPGA Tour members tying for 2nd place, not exempt, in a cumulative money list taken from the USPGA Tour Players Championship and the five USPGA Tour events leading up to and including the 2006 Western Open.

(16) The leading player, not exempt having applied (15) above, in the first 10 and ties of each of the 2006 Buick Championship, the 2006 Western Open and the 2006 John Deere Classic. Ties will be decided by the better final round score and, if still tied, by the better third round score and then by the better second round score. If still tied, a hole by hole card playoff will take place starting at the 18th hole of the final round.

(17) Playing members of the 2005 Presidents Cup teams.

(18) First and anyone tying for 1st place on the Order of Merit of the Asian Tour for 2005.

(19) First 2 and anyone tying for 2nd place on the Order of Merit of the Tour of Australasia for 2005.

(20) First and anyone tying for 1st place on the Order of Merit of the Southern Africa PGA Sunshine Tour for 2005/2006.

(21) The Canadian Open Champion for 2005.

(22) The Japan Open Champion for 2005.

(23) First 2 and anyone tying for 2nd place, not exempt, on the Official Money List of the Japan Golf Tour for 2005.

(24) The leading 4 players, not exempt, in the 2006 Mizuno Open. Ties will be decided by the better final round score and, if still tied, by the better third round score and then by the better second round score. If still tied, a hole by hole card playoff will take place starting at the 18th hole of the final round.

(25) First 2 and anyone tying for 2nd place, not exempt having applied (24) above, in a cumulative money list taken from all official Japan Golf Tour events from the 2006 Japan PGA Championship up to and including the 2006 Mizuno Open.

(26) The Senior British Open Champion for 2005.

(27) The Amateur Champion for 2006.

(28) The US Amateur Champion for 2005.

(29) The European Individual Amateur Champion for 2005.

(27) to (29) are only applicable if the entrant concerned is still an amateur on 20 July 2006.

Local Final Qualifying
10-11 July

Conwy (Caernarvonshire)

Jon Bevan, England	73	66	139
Warren Bladon, England	70	72	142
Mikko Ilonen, Finland	69	73	142

Formby

Jim Payne, England	67	71	138
Andrew Marshall, England	69	70	139
Darren Parris, England	69	70	139

Wallasey

Gary Day, England	67	72	139
*Danny Denison, England	70	69	139
Markus Brier, Austria	74	67	141

West Lancashire

Nick Ludwell, England	72	68	140
Gary Lockerbie, England	73	68	141
Adam Frayne, England	69	73	142

Denotes amateur

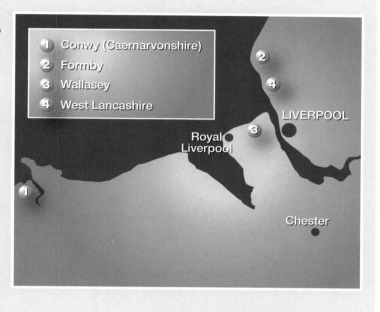

1. Conwy (Caernarvonshire)
2. Formby
3. Wallasey
4. West Lancashire

The Starting Field

"G(1) In the event of an exempt player withdrawing from the Championship or further places becoming available in the starting field after IFQ Europe and IFQ America, these places will be allocated in ranking order of entrants from the Official World Golf Ranking at the time that intimation of the withdrawal is received by the Championship Committee. Any withdrawals following the issue of OWGR Week 27 will be taken in ranking order from OWGR Week 27."

Gonzalo Fernandez-Castano replaced Greg Norman
Jeff Sluman replaced David Toms

Simon Khan replaced Justin Leonard
Andrew Buckle replaced Trevor Immelman

Jon Bevan

Jim Payne

Gary Day

Nick Ludwell

International Final Qualifying

ASIA   6-7 April

Sentosa   *Singapore*

Jarrod Lyle, Australia	67	71	138
Unho Park, Australia	68	70	138
(P)Shiv Kahur, India	69	70	139

Jarrod Lyle

AMERICA   26 June

Congressional   *Bethesda, Maryland*

Note: Due to cancellation because of weather, the qualifying places were allocated to players in the starting field in Official World Golf Ranking Week 25 order.

	OWGR#25
Tom Pernice Jnr, USA	54
Brett Wetterich, USA	55
Vaughn Taylor, USA	57
Lee Westwood, England	59
Greg Owen, England	64
Bo Van Pelt, USA	67
J B Holmes, USA	71
Jerry Kelly, USA	73
Ted Purdy, USA	74
Steve Elkington, Australia	75
Jeff Maggert, USA	77
Aaron Baddeley, Australia	78

Tom Pernice Jnr.

AUSTRALASIA   31 Jan -1 Feb

Kingston Heath   *Melbourne, Australia*

Michael Wright, Australia	69	66	135
Bradley Hughes, Australia	69	69	138
Ben Bunny, Australia	69	69	138
Adam Bland, Australia	73	66	139

Michael Wright

EUROPE — 26 June

Sunningdale — *Berkshire, England*

Player	R1	R2	Total
Louis Oosthuizen, South Africa	66	66	132
Marco Ruiz, Paraguay	67	65	132
Richard Green, Australia	69	66	135
Sam Little, England	69	66	135
Mark Pilkington, Wales	69	66	135
Soren Kjeldsen, Denmark	68	68	136
Barry Lane, England	68	68	136
Carlos Rodiles, Spain	68	68	136
Simon Wakefield, England	67	69	136
Jamie Donaldson, Wales	67	70	137
Peter Hedblom, Sweden	70	67	137
Phillip Price, Wales	70	67	137
Brett Rumford, Australia	66	71	137
Lee Slattery, England	70	67	137
(P)Simon Dyson, England	71	67	138
(P)Graeme McDowell, N. Ireland	69	69	138
(P)Robert Rock, England	68	70	138
(P)Richard Sterne, South Africa	71	67	138

Louis Oosthuizen

Hoylake

AFRICA — 18-19 January

Royal Johannesburg & Kensington — *Johannesburg, South Africa*

Player	R1	R2	Total
Warren Abery, South Africa	66	70	136
Ross Wellington, South Africa	69	68	137
Bruce Vaughan, USA	69	69	138
Thomas Aiken, South Africa	71	67	138

Warren Abery

Welcome Back To Hoylake

By Andy Farrell

An eagle at the 18th gave Tiger Woods a solid beginning to the defence of his title, but a young Irishman took the honours in The Open's joyful return to Royal Liverpool.

A man walked into a pub, as all the best jokes start. The 135th Open Championship began the same way. It was a light-hearted moment with prophetic repercussions. On the evening of the hottest day so far of Britain's summer heat wave, a man walked into a hostelry named La Bodega in Hoylake and amid the throng spotted someone he recognised already enjoying the atmosphere.

"You're Graeme McDowell, aren't you?" he asked. McDowell, in relaxed mood despite a major championship starting the following morning, replied in the affirmative and got ready to provide an autograph. Instead, the man said: "You get pretty laid

Graeme McDowell scored six birdies and no bogeys.

off at the top of your backswing, don't you?"

"Yeah, I guess I do," McDowell responded, momentarily caught off guard. "Get a bit of work done on that, will you," persisted the local before, advice dispensed, he went on his way. "It was pretty funny," McDowell recalled. "Fair play, to him, he knew his stuff. It's something I'm working on anyway. I was joking with the guys I was with that if I shot 66 in the next day I'd want to see him on the range on Friday."

The least he could have done was buy the mystery consultant a beer since scoring a 66 was exactly what McDowell did the next day to lead The Open after the first round. As McDowell's name appeared at the top of the leaderboard, he could not help but think of Fred Daly, a Portrush man like McDowell who remains the only Irishman to have won The Open.

Daly won at Hoylake in 1947 and already it was clear that The Open returning to the Royal Liverpool Golf Club for the first time in 39 years was going to be a success. Few places ooze history quite the way the links of Hoylake does and it made for a potent blend with the masters of the modern game.

A fascinating opening day climaxed with Tiger Woods holing an eagle putt on the 18th green. Suddenly Woods, after a 67, had finished the day only a stroke behind McDowell and alongside two Englishmen, Greg Owen and Anthony Wall, Miguel Angel Jimenez, of Spain, and Japan's Keiichiro Fukabori. A large group stood on 68, four under par,

The mowers were out on the greens before dawn.

that included Ernie Els, Sergio Garcia, Jim Furyk, Mike Weir, and Adam Scott. By mutual consent the sight of the defending champion celebrating with a clenched fist pump on the final green could only be described as "ominous."

Perhaps the only moment that was more dramatic on this opening Thursday came hours earlier at first light. The oppressive conditions finally broke with a thunderstorm accompanied by heavy rain. At 5.40 am, it was decided that there was still enough electrical activity around that the first tee time of 6.30 would be delayed by half an hour. Sweden's Peter Hedblom struck the first ball at 7 am and immediately the interest was in how the conditions had changed the course.

After days and days of heat the course had been baked to a light brown colour and was playing as hard and fast as any Open venue in recent memory. It would have taken a deluge of Biblical proportions

Thursday Weather
Rain early morning, then a bright sunny day with a light westerly breeze.

After a weather delay of 30 minutes, Peter Hedblom was first off at precisely 7 am in The Open Championship 2006.

to alter the fundamental characteristics, but the sight of the odd pitch mark for the first time in the week was a welcome one for the early starters. Approach shots no longer needed to be landed short of the greens and, after the storm, it was calm. Later on, as the sun came out and the breeze picked up, the course soon reverted to type. So the early starters had an advantage? "What do you think, mate?" said Els.

Els was one of the few players to have played competitively at Hoylake before. Indeed, the South African was a winner over the course, having triumphed as a young amateur in the Tillman Trophy in 1988. A photograph hangs in the entrance hall of the clubhouse showing Els with the trophy and plenty of youthful, energetic hair. It was safe to say the mature Els was slightly embarrassed about the picture, even before Nick Faldo said he looked like a "toilet brush."

Part of the intrigue about this week concerned the

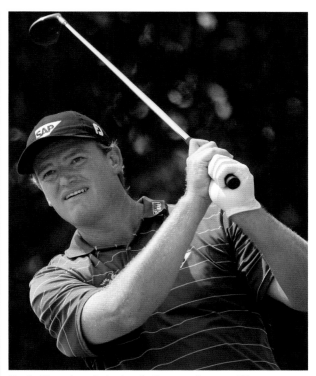

Ernie Els enjoyed playing in the morning conditions.

First Round Leaders

HOLE	1	2	3	4	5	6	7	8	9	10	11	12	13	14	15	16	17	18	
PAR	**4**	**4**	**4**	**4**	**5**	**3**	**4**	**4**	**3**	**5**	**4**	**4**	**3**	**4**	**3**	**5**	**4**	**5**	**TOTAL**
Graeme McDowell	4	4	4	4	(4)	3	(3)	4	(2)	(4)	(3)	4	3	4	3	(4)	4	5	66
Greg Owen	4	4	4	4	(4)	3	4	(3)	3	5	4	[5]	(2)	(3)	3	(4)	4	(4)	67
Anthony Wall	4	4	4	4	(4)	3	(3)	4	3	(3)	[5]	4	(2)	4	3	(3)	[5]	5	67
Miguel Angel Jimenez	4	4	4	[5]	(4)	3	4	(3)	(2)	(4)	4	4	3	4	3	(4)	4	(4)	67
Keiichiro Fukabori	[5]	4	4	4	(4)	(2)	4	(3)	3	(4)	4	4	(2)	[5]	(2)	(4)	[5]	(4)	67
Tiger Woods	[5]	4	4	4	(4)	3	4	4	(2)	5	(3)	4	3	4	3	(4)	4	(3)	67
Marcus Fraser	4	4	4	4	(4)	3	4	4	(2)	(4)	4	4	(2)	[5]	3	(4)	[5]	(4)	68
S K Ho	4	(3)	4	4	(4)	3	4	(3)	3	(4)	4	4	3	[5]	3	(4)	4	5	68
Mikko Ilonen	4	4	4	4	5	(2)	4	(3)	3	(4)	4	4	3	4	3	(4)	[5]	(4)	68
Mark Hensby	4	4	[7]	(3)	(4)	3	4	(3)	(2)	(4)	(3)	[5]	3	(3)	3	(4)	[5]	(4)	68
Sergio Garcia	(3)	4	4	4	(4)	3	(3)	4	3	5	4	4	3	[5]	3	(4)	4	(4)	68
Mike Weir	[5]	(3)	[5]	(3)	(4)	3	4	4	3	(4)	4	4	(2)	4	3	(4)	4	5	68
Ernie Els	[5]	(3)	(3)	4	5	3	4	4	3	(4)	[5]	4	(2)	(3)	3	(4)	4	5	68
Jim Furyk	4	[5]	(3)	4	(4)	3	4	(3)	3	(4)	4	4	3	[5]	3	(4)	4	(4)	68
Tom Lehman	4	4	4	(3)	5	3	(3)	4	3	(4)	4	4	3	4	3	5	4	(4)	68
Carl Pettersson	4	[6]	4	4	(4)	3	4	[5]	3	(4)	(3)	4	3	4	(2)	(4)	(3)	(4)	68
Adam Scott	4	(3)	[5]	4	(4)	3	4	(3)	3	[6]	(3)	4	(2)	4	3	(3)	[5]	5	68
Ben Crane	[5]	4	4	(3)	(4)	3	4	4	3	(4)	4	4	(2)	4	[4]	(4)	4	(4)	68
Brett Rumford	(3)	[5]	4	(3)	(3)	3	4	4	3	(4)	4	4	[4]	(3)	[4]	(4)	4	5	68

1

In the Words of the Competitors...

❝

"There was a lot of rain last night which softened the course considerably. In the practice rounds, we were landing short of the green, and today you could easily land four or five metres on the green."

—Marcus Fraser

"I got off to a good start, and then I made a triple bogey on No 3, and then came back and played decently. That's about it."

—Mark Hensby

"Definitely I know that I still have to work on my game. Don't get me wrong, it's a very nice round, but I'm still not fully satisfied."

—Sergio Garcia

"The greens I felt were tough to judge the speed, because there's some green spots out there and some bigger spots, and you end up putting through both of them, trying to judge what the ball is going to do."

—Mike Weir

"It's a great golf course. It's so bunkered. It gives you all kinds of options."

—Ernie Els

"It was just one of those days. I couldn't do much right."

—Padraig Harrington

lack of anyone in the field who had previously played in an Open at Hoylake. In addition to Els, others had some amateur experience over the links, including Padraig Harrington at the 1993 Home Internationals, David Howell at the 1995 Amateur Championship, and in the same event five years later, Aaron Baddeley, the Liverpool-born Nick Dougherty, and the winner, Mikko Ilonen. The last European Tour event to be staged at Hoylake was the 1991 European Pro-Celebrity, which was won by Paul Broadhurst. The following week he finished second in the German Open to qualify for the Ryder Cup team. Now, 15 years later, Broadhurst was having a fine season and hoping for a return to the team for the first time since.

Quite how the scoring would go was another fascination. It promised to be good, given the conditions and the rough having been burnt off by the fierce sun of recent weeks. But prophecies of the first 62 scored in a major championship and other scoring records being broken appeared as sensationalised as the comments in the American magazine *Golf Digest* that the course was a "thing of the past" and not up to hosting a modern championship. There was talk of players coming up in the months prior to The Open and knocking it round in low numbers with hardly a care in the world. Harrington had the answer. "The thing about a links course, more than other courses, is that you only find out how hard they are when you are playing in competition," he said.

In only the second group, Australian Marcus Fraser scored the first 68 of the day. In the group behind, Ilonen and S K Ho did

Marcus Fraser returned the first 68, and 12 more would follow.

Mikko Ilonen recalled a longer, greener course.

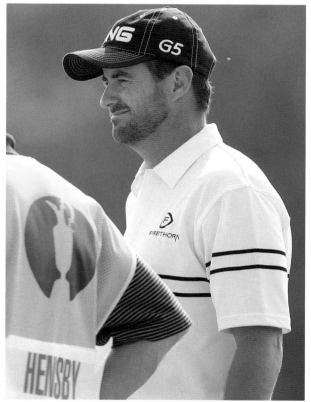

Mark Hensby overcame an early blunder.

likewise. For Ilonen, from Finland, it was a pleasant return to Hoylake for the first time since he won the Amateur in 2000. Fraser got up at 4.20 am. "I thought it was like getting up at home to watch when I was a kid," he said. "There were a lot of early mornings getting up to watch Greg Norman and the guys."

Fraser birdied all four of the par-5s, which seemed to confirm the theory that scoring, at least in relation to par, would be good. But if there were rewards for good golf to be found, poor shots could be severely punished. Unusually, Hoylake has internal out of bounds, specifically at the third and the 18th holes. (For the purposes of historical comparison, and for those who know Hoylake through its many amateur competitions, it should be pointed out that the traditional doglegged first hole, with the out of bounds on the right all the way up to the green,

became the third because the 16th was here used as the finishing hole, and the normal 17th and 18th as the first and second. If controversial when first announced, the renumbering proved a success over the week.)

Mark Hensby, another of the record crop of 23 Australians in the field, soon discovered to his cost that going right with his approach at the third was not allowed. A triple-bogey 7 resulted, but he responded with nine birdies to join the group at 68. "I admit I got pretty angry," he said. "I free-wheeled a bit from there and that got me back on track."

There were no such problems for Els or Garcia, although Els three-putted at the first hole before birdieing the next two holes to get back on an even keel. The feeling was Els could not have shot any higher than 68, and Garcia, too, missed some

1

chances to go lower. He three-putted at the par-5 10th hole and missed a short putt at the 13th. "Those things stopped my momentum," said the young Spaniard. "If I could roll my potato nicely, that would be good."

Weir started with two bogeys and three birdies in the first five holes, while Furyk matched his four-under effort. Of the players who came close to winning the US Open at Winged Foot the previous month, Furyk had the best return here. Harrington, who bogeyed the last three holes in New York, started with a double bogey after driving into a bunker and limped in with a 75 which he immediately acknowledged gave him little to no chance.

Of course, both Phil Mickelson and Colin Montgomerie took double bogeys at the 72nd hole to hand the US Open trophy to Geoff Ogilvy. How they would react was one topic of conversation. Monty birdied the first hole but his round stuttered with bogeys at the 12th and the 13th, the latter from three-putting. Ironically, it was on the same green a couple of evenings earlier that he had spent hours practising his putting in a recreation of a similar routine that propelled him to second place at St Andrews in 2005.

But after a 73, the Scot was despondent. "I never got the pace of the greens," Montgomerie said. At one point his post-round interview almost turned into the Two Ronnies sketch about the Mastermind contestant replying to a question with the answer to the next question. "How..." "very" "frustrating..." "very" "was it..." "very" "given the amount of practice..." "VERY" "you have done?"

Mickelson fared better, although the left-hander faded a touch after a bright start for a 69. His first

It took six holes for Mike Weir to record his first par, but his 68 included three birdies and no bogeys after that.

Perhaps It Is Pride That Drives Ballesteros

Three-Times Open Champion Plays Better Than Anyone Expected

Javier and Seve Ballesteros

Pride can be a very powerful force—in yourself and your performance, in your son and in your family name. Perhaps it was pride that made Severiano Ballesteros compete at Hoylake for the first time in an Open for five years and perhaps it was pride again that enabled the 1979, 1984, and 1988 Open champion to play better than we had dared hope and better than he had expected.

There were fears that Ballesteros might go round in 81 as he had in the French Open in June. One 81 would be bad enough but two 81s, as had happened at Le Golf National three weeks earlier? It didn't bear thinking about.

Nothing Ballesteros did in practice removed these nagging worries. He kept to himself, playing each day with Javier, his 15-year-old son, as his caddie, admitting that he felt he did not have the game to compete in The Open. On the 14th hole on Wednesday, during a practice round with Sandy Lyle, Ballesteros hit three shots at the green; all three missed, two were short, one went left.

But then Ballesteros confounded us all. The figures are that he went out in 36, came home in 38, and thus went round in 74, two over par, two strokes more than Shaun Micheel, one less than Ian Poulter, his playing companions.

It was not pretty, but those who remembered Ballesteros playing against Tom Lehman in the 1995 Ryder Cup knew that 11 years later, aged 49 and with an arthritic back and out of tournament practice, Ballesteros was likely to be worse not better. Towards the end of his round he demonstrated that the genius he always had in his hands had not diminished. Three times in his last four holes he single-putted. Twice within four holes he needed to drop his ball without penalty because of wild approach shots. On both occasions, the 15th and 18th, he chipped to within a putter's length of the hole and sank the putt for his par. He one-putted eight greens.

"I've never played with anyone who has a better short game," Poulter said. "Jose Maria [Olazabal] comes close, but he is nothing like Seve. The chips he played were pure brilliance. I've never seen anyone with softer hands. How he gets the ball to land so softly is amazing."

The moment that summed it all up came when Ballesteros stood with one foot in and one foot outside a bunker on the 16th. Somehow he got the ball out to the position on the green where he knew it would run to within 10 or 12 feet of the flagstick. From there he holed the putt, inevitably.

"To walk the fairways of The Open Championship alongside my son was fantastic," Ballesteros said, giving a good explanation as to why he had managed to play so much better than anyone had expected. "He is a very good player and learned a lot of things today. Especially how to accept losing shots from bad shots."

—**John Hopkins**

After his 73, Colin Montgomerie said he had 'a bit of hard work to do,' and he admitted to being very frustrated.

On his disappointing 74, Luke Donald said, 'It was a frustrating day, as it was a great chance to post a good score.'

nine contained five 3s, including a birdie at the first and an eagle at the fifth. He was four under after 10 holes, but inexplicably putted off the green at the 12th and dropped another shot at the 14th.

Montgomerie and Harrington were not the only home players to struggle. David Howell, the winner of the BMW PGA Championship at Wentworth, had signed his autograph on page 110 of the official programme often enough to notice, if he should need reminding, that he had not made a cut in The Open for seven years. He needed a good start, but drove out of bounds at the 18th and finished with a 74.

Luke Donald and local hero Dougherty were also on 74, while Ian Poulter had a 75, including a triple bogey at the 14th. One of his playing partners was Seve Ballesteros, playing for the first time in five years. Seve was impressed with Poulter's outfit, the union flag on his shirt and the Claret Jug on his red trousers. "I thought he looked like a matador, though really he should not have been wearing red, for that is rather attractive to the bull," Ballesteros said.

Instead, it was Greg Owen, playing with Furyk, who took the early clubhouse lead with a 67. Despite a back injury that required atten-

Low Scores	
Low First Nine	
S K Ho	32
Sergio Garcia	32
Phil Mickelson	32
Sean O'Hair	32
Brandt Jobe	32
Graeme McDowell	32
Aaron Baddeley	32
Brett Rumford	32
Low Second Nine	
Carl Pettersson	31
Low Round	
Graeme McDowell	66

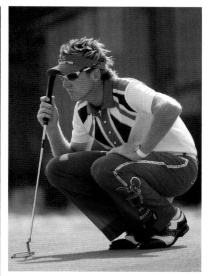

Even after a 67, Greg Owen was reminded of his Bay Hill meltdown.

Ian Poulter 'looked like a matador.'

tion from the physiotherapists twice a day, Owen followed a bogey at the 12th with birdies at the 13th, 14th, 16th, and 18th holes. Owen heralds from the Coxmoor club in Nottinghamshire, about two hours away, but plays mainly in the United States. In what was not the only grouping that raised eyebrows, as well as Furyk, Owen played with Rod Pampling, the Australian who won the Bay Hill Invitational in March when Owen suffered a horrific putting meltdown on the 71st green. "No, we didn't talk about it," Owen said with a smile.

Anthony Wall, the son of a retired London black cab driver, joined Owen on five under after becoming the only player to have two eagles. He holed from 25 feet at the 10th and then hit a five iron to two feet at the 16th. That put him at six under, but he dropped a shot at the 17th and could not birdie the last. As a young amateur he had practised next to Nick Faldo on the range at Sunningdale and was never afraid to pick the brain of the great man. Being thrust into the limelight now in only his second major championship was not something he was overly concerned about. "I've got two young kids," he said. "I'll be changing nappies in an hour."

McDowell achieved what only Tom Lehman, during a 68, could also manage, which was not to drop a shot. His preparations at the course, along with his coach, Claude Harmon, had started the previous Sunday. "When I turned on the TV this morning I was worried that the last four days had been a waste of time, but by the time we were playing there was not much difference in the course," said the 26-year-old Northern Irishman.

It's a Fact

Before this year the lowest rounds in The Open at Royal Liverpool were the 67s in the third round of 1967 by the eventual champion, Roberto de Vicenzo, and Gary Player. Other scores below 70 in The Open's history at Royal Liverpool were the 68s in the first round by D F Smalldon in 1956 and Lionel Platts in 1967, the 68 in the fourth round by Hugh Boyle in 1967, and the 69s in the second round by Jack Nicklaus, Tony Jacklin, R R W Davenport, and Harry Weetman in 1967.

In the Words of the Competitors...

"No one really knows how to play here. There have been no big events here for quite some time. But it is a quality golf course, and if you play well you will score well."

—Anthony Wall

"I hit some poor shots coming in and put the ball in a few spots I didn't want to be, and it cost me a few strokes. But I'm three under, we've got three rounds left, and I'll see if I can make some more birdies this week-end."

—Phil Mickelson

"There are a lot of Korean women golfers doing very well. This week it is time to show how well the men can play too."

—S K Ho

"Maybe I need to come over earlier. This time I came over a little earlier, and I'm just trying to find the right recipe."

—Jim Furyk

"I drove it into just about every bunker. Those are hazards you can't afford to go into, and I found too many of them."

—Luke Donald

Bogeys on the par-4 Nos. 12 and 14 left Phil Mickelson at three under par.

Anthony Wall posted two eagles on the inward nine.

Amateur champion Julien Guerrier had a 72 to start.

McDowell's previous best round in a major championship was the 67 with which he tied for 11th in The Open at St Andrews in 2005. One shot less and he would have qualified automatically for a place at Hoylake. Instead, McDowell had to go to the International Final Qualifying at Sunningdale. There he holed a 25-foot putt for a birdie on the final green to get into a seven-man playoff. Four spots were available the following morning when the players returned to the course, and McDowell managed to nab one of them.

Due to the modifications to the course, his 66 stood as a new course record and, in any case, he eclipsed by one stroke the lowest ever scored in an Open at Hoylake. His first birdie came at the par-5 fifth, then another at the par-4 seventh, and he holed a bunker shot at the ninth to be out in 32. He holed from 12 feet at the 11th, but otherwise

SK Ho said he had learned 'to manage a links.'

Clarke Puts Golf Clubs Aside
Other players express sympathy and support

After posting his score of 69 on the first day, Darren Clarke stated that The Open Championship would be his last tournament "for the foreseeable future." His wife, Heather, a cancer victim for five years, was growing weaker and he wanted to be at her side.

(Editor's Note: Heather Clarke passed away on 13 August.)

At the Smurfit European Open at The K Club, a couple of weeks earlier, Clarke had spoken of how he had no option but to keep on grinding with his golf; that he could not throw in the towel. When someone who had seen the suffering on his face all season asked why he felt like that, Clarke paused for a moment before delivering a reply from the heart. "There's no point," he said, "in giving up on anything."

There had been a pattern to Clarke's scoring in the weeks leading up to The Open. He would play great golf over the first two days before slipping from the leaderboard at the weekend. The Barclays Scottish Open was a case in point. He began with rounds of 66 and 65 before adding scores of 71 and 72.

Clarke could explain it. He said that he was on automatic pilot in the early stages of a tournament and that that worked well enough until the pressure began to mount. Then, as he pushed to finish the job, "my mind goes all over the place."

That was the case again here, and Clarke left Hoylake after his 82 in the second round.

At the start of The Open week, Tiger Woods, whose father died from cancer in May, gave his take on what was happening to his Irish friend. From his experience, Clarke would be feeling completely drained. After a couple of rounds, he would have nothing left to give.

Before The Open, Clarke had been given some practical advice to set alongside the sympathy. Conor O'Brien, doctor to the Irish Olympic team and a member at Portmarnock, had rung him on the previous Sunday evening to say that he had been watching his last round at Loch Lomond and noted that he was showing all the symptoms of being badly dehydrated. He told him to take plenty of isotonic drinks on board.

Clarke thrived on that advice in his opening round at Royal Liverpool, while he also thrived on the links golf to which he had been born. "This course is fantastic," he said. "It's pure, links golf. It's as

Darren Clarke started with a 69.

good as it gets." Warming to his theme, he talked of how "you can putt it from 40 yards, chip it, hit a five iron, do whatever you want."

The feeling was that if there were any venue which was going to help him to keep going for all 72 holes at so desperate a time in his life, this was it. Again, it did no harm to his cause that people were backing him body and soul.

Colin Montgomerie, it seemed, had been speaking for all the European contingent when he said halfway through the Barclays Scottish Open, "With what Darren's been going through, I'd be happy to finish second to him."

—Lewine Mair

Miguel Angel Jimenez had only one dropped shot, at the par-4 fourth, followed by six birdies.

Ten years after his Open victory, Tom Lehman was pleased with his four birdies.

two-putted for birdies at the 10th and the 16th. It was a fine round of golf from tee-to-green, never getting himself in major trouble. "I didn't exactly light up the world with my putter," he said. "Hopefully, I've saved a few of those for the weekend."

Overall the scoring was not quite as good in the afternoon, but Jimenez was five under for the last 11 holes and Fukabori made 2s at three of the four short holes to finish one behind McDowell. Adam Scott might have joined them but for 5s at the last two holes, so he went into the pack at four under with American Ben Crane, Australia's Brett Rumford, and Sweden's Carl Pettersson, who birdied the last four holes.

Chris DiMarco started his round well, with three birdies in the first four holes, and finished it well, with three birdies in the last four holes, but in between took a triple-bogey 7 at the seventh. He drove into a bush and took two hacks to get out and even then only into a bunker. Had he taken an unplayable, the result might have been different. Not just of that hole, or his first round of 70, but of the whole championship.

All the good golf at least distracted from what had been built up as the main contest of the day. Shingo Katayama must have wondered what he had stepped into when he was drawn with Woods and Faldo. In his new job as a commentator on American television, Faldo had managed to upset Woods 18 months earlier, and until a greeting on the practice putting green on Wednesday, the American

Excerpts FROM THE **Press**

"They followed in their thousands, each hoping for a glimpse of the past and the chance to say that they had seen in person one of the most flamboyant and exciting golfers the world has ever seen. No, not Ian Poulter. Severiano Ballesteros."

—Peter Dixon, *The Times*

"One of the early leaders, Finland's Mikko Ilonen, had felt emboldened to say the course was very easy, but Lee Westwood knows better than to act so cocksure."

—Oliver Brown, *The Daily Telegraph*

"Sergio Garcia's Open hopes are no longer paella in the sky—thanks to his mum's delicious home cooking. Garcia has rented a massive house on the Wirral this week and turned the occasion into a family fiesta."

—Iain MacFarlane, *Daily Star*

"American skipper Tom Lehman carded a fine 68 and revealed that lots of the fans who followed his group only wanted to talk about the Ryder Cup."

—Dick Turner, *Daily Sport*

"They were flying in from all directions, storylines emerging as if carried by the winds of the nearby Irish Sea. Ernie Els made some noise, finally. Sergio Garcia planted himself in early contention. Graeme McDowell fired a record round. Then shortly after 7 pm, as the warmth of a summer day slowly gave way to dusk, none other than Tiger Woods loudly announced his presence at Royal Liverpool."

—Ron Kroichick, *San Francisco Chronicle*

Round of the Day

OFFICIAL SCORECARD
THE OPEN CHAMPIONSHIP 2006
ROYAL LIVERPOOL GOLF CLUB, HOYLAKE

FOR R&A USE ONLY 34.3   ROUND 1
18 HOLE TOTAL

Graeme McDOWELL

Game 34
Thursday 20 July at 12:58 pm

THIS ROUND 66   66

VERIFIED

ROUND 1

Hole	1	2	3	4	5	6	7	8	9	Out
Yards	454	436	429	372	528	202	453	423	198	3495
Par	4	4	4	4	5	3	4	4	3	35
Score	4	4	4	4	4	3	3	4	2	32

	10	11	12	13	14	15	16	17	18	In	Total
Yards	534	393	448	198	456	161	554	459	560	3763	7258
Par	5	4	4	3	4	3	5	4	5	37	72
Score	4	3	4	3	4	3	4	4	5	34	66

Signature of Marker

Signature of Competitor — Graeme McDowell

Extra preparation under the supervision of his coach paid off for Graeme McDowell in the first round of The Open Championship. He played 27 holes each day on Sunday and Monday. "I was playing a lot of shots around the greens and doing a lot of experimentation and trying different shots that I was going to require," McDowell said. "I felt very, very prepared for the week."

McDowell's round of 66, six under par, was the low score of the first day, and came without a bogey. He reached the par-5 fifth hole with a drive and four iron to 15 feet and two putts. He scored a birdie on a putt of eight feet at the par-4 seventh and holed out from a bunker on the par-3 ninth. On the inward nine, McDowell reached the par-5 10th hole in two and took two putts. He holed from 12 feet on the par-4 11th and two-putted from 15 feet on the par-5 16th.

"I feel like I can control the ball very well," McDowell said. "I hit some nice irons and gave myself some nice chances. I didn't light up the world with my putter, but I've certainly been rolling it well lately.

"I feel like I've really been getting very close to some of my top form."

had not seemed to want to let it go.

Under the microscope they shook hands on the first tee and the 18th green and between times they each did what he now does best: Faldo talked and Tiger played golf. Faldo, admitting he was rusty from so little practice, shot a 77; Woods was 10 strokes better. In only his seventh competitive round since April and the death of his father, Earl, in early May, Tiger started slowly.

He three-putted the first green and took two to escape from a horrid lie under the face of a bunker at the 10th. Birdies at the fifth and the ninth, however, meant an outward 34, and he would come home

Players Below Par	67
Players At Par	24
Players Above Par	65

Tiger Woods celebrated when his putt for eagle-3 on No. 18 fell into the hole.

Excerpts
FROM THE Press

"First blood to Europe, although the quickening pulse says there is so much to come. And, naturally, nobody is pumping it more furiously than Tiger Woods. This enthralling first day of The Open Championship will rightfully be remembered for his punch in the air on the final green that took him to within one of Northern Ireland's Graeme McDowell."

—James Corrigan, *The Independent*

"Perhaps only in this part of the world would a punter have the nerve to go up to a top golfer in a pub, the cheek to tell him what he is doing wrong, and the knowledge to be proved right. Somewhere in Hoylake last night Graeme McDowell was looking to buy the man a drink."

—Derek Lawrenson, *Daily Mail*

"Tiger Woods, who had a two-month layoff earlier this summer because of the death of his father, spent much of the afternoon groping for his best game and scrambling to get himself out of trouble."

—Oliver Holt, *Daily Mirror*

"The lowest representation of Scots in Open Championship history was compounded by an underwhelming start from the four hopefuls. The quartet all failed to finish under par after the first round to leave themselves with much work to be done."

—Martin Greig, *The Herald*

Lee Westwood birdied the 16th and 18th holes to be three under par.

in 33 to allay any fears of a repeat of his missing the cut at the US Open. In his opening practice round at Hoylake, Woods had found he could hit his driver over 370 yards on the fast-running fairways.

"But there was no way to control the ball," Woods said. "Although the rough is wispy, you don't want to be in it, even hitting a wedge." So the game plan was to keep the ball on the fairway and, as at the Old Course, where he had won twice, to avoid the bunkers. More often than not he wanted to be short of the bunkers, so he took his five wood out of the bag and replaced it with a two iron for the first time in the season. Over the next four days he would wear out that club. Occasionally, he would hit a three wood off the tee, as he did at the 11th, where he missed the fairway on the right but still managed to make a birdie.

He might as well have taken out the driver, for only once, on the 16th hole in the first round, did he hit it. Otherwise it remained sweatily under its tiger headcover. "Even that I wasn't supposed to do," he said of the one time he did bring out the big stick. "But the wind was down at that moment and I felt it took the bunkers out of play, which it did." He went on to birdie there and then came to the last. He hit a two iron off the tee at a hole measuring 560 yards and had 256 to the flag for his second shot. He hit a four iron and finished just past pin-high right of the flag in the middle of the green. In went the putt.

"It was a nice couple of shots and a good way to finish," Woods said. "I was watching on television in the morning and someone else had that putt and it doesn't break. I hit it right-edge and it held its line."

This was not the last of the drama on the 18th green. Over two hours later, well past 9.30 pm, the last group finished their rounds in style. South African Ross Wellington had a 30-foot putt for an eagle and Englishmen Darren Parris and Sam Little both birdied, all applauded by about 10 people, mostly greenkeepers and rubbish collectors.

Woods had enjoyed a more fitting ovation. There were 67 rounds under par. Clearly, however, Tiger's was the most significant. It was the fourth time he had opened with a round in the 60s at The Open. A 65 at Royal Birkdale in 1998 led to a third-place finish. But a 67 in 2000 and a 66 in 2005, both at St Andrews, led to victories.

Ross Wellington finished with an eagle.

Round One Hole Summary

HOLE	PAR	YARDS	EAGLES	BIRDIES	PARS	BOGEYS	D.BOGEYS	HIGHER	RANK	AVERAGE
1	4	454	0	18	99	33	6	0	8	4.17
2	4	436	0	17	88	45	5	1	4	4.26
3	4	429	0	13	103	35	3	2	5	4.22
4	4	372	0	20	116	18	2	0	12	4.01
5	5	528	7	72	65	10	2	0	16	4.54
6	3	202	0	5	118	29	4	0	6	3.21
7	4	453	0	23	91	34	7	1	7	4.18
8	4	423	0	23	114	15	3	1	13	4.01
9	3	198	0	26	100	26	3	1	10	3.06
OUT	**35**	**3495**	**7**	**217**	**894**	**245**	**35**	**6**		**35.65**
10	5	534	5	91	49	7	4	0	17	4.45
11	4	393	0	20	111	24	1	0	11	4.04
12	4	448	0	1	91	57	6	1	1	4.46
13	3	198	0	23	99	33	0	1	9	3.08
14	4	456	0	9	95	45	5	2	2	4.33
15	3	161	0	20	117	17	2	0	13	3.01
16	5	554	12	93	43	8	0	0	18	4.30
17	4	459	0	11	93	49	3	0	3	4.28
18	5	560	4	70	68	10	3	1	15	4.62
IN	**37**	**3763**	**21**	**338**	**766**	**250**	**24**	**5**		**36.57**
TOTAL	**72**	**7258**	**28**	**555**	**1660**	**495**	**59**	**11**		**72.22**

Excerpts FROM THE Press

"Caddies and golfers are not the only people suffering in the heat at Hoylake this week. The R&A has kitted out marshals in smart red sleeveless fleeces, perfect for normal links conditions but hardly ideal for the scorching temperatures on the course this week."

—**Paul Kelso, *The Guardian***

"Lee Slattery marked his first appearance in The Open by producing what he described last night as 'the round of my life.' The Southport golfer returned a three-under-par 69 on the opening day."

—**Richard Williamson,
*Liverpool Daily Post***

"Luke Donald promised much after coming into The Open having finished second at Loch Lomond, but the Ryder Cup hero came a cropper and will have to post a round in the 60s to ensure that he is still there for the weekend."

—**Niall Hickman, *Daily Express***

"Padraig Harrington was gutted after a dismal opening-round 75—leaving him with a mountain to climb. The Dubliner, who started sixth favourite at 18-1, believes he has too much ground to make up."

—**Steven Howard, *The Sun***

"Jim Furyk may be a former US Open champion and the No 5-ranked player in the world, but he also has missed the cut the last five times he has played in The Open, a mysterious run that seems likely to end on Friday."

—**Leonard Shapiro,
*The Washington Post***

Caddie Simon Clarke pointed the line of the shot to Keiichirio Fukabori.

A mobile cameraman followed Rod Pampling (left) and Jim Furyk.

Graeme McDowell
Off And Running In The Open

By Mike Aitken

In other sports, such as football, professional athletes who visit the pub for a drink with friends and find themselves recognised by the public, are either asked for autographs or subjected to good-natured banter. Only in golf is the man who led the first round of The Open given an astute technical tip by a punter on how to play even better.

Graeme McDowell, the young Ulsterman who showed the rest of the field the way at Royal Liverpool when he eliminated any mistakes from his score and carded six birdies in an opening round of 66, recounted the story of walking into La Bodega, a bar around the corner from the train station in Hoylake, and being approached by a local man.

"It's a pretty nice spot where many people hang out in the evenings," reported the 26-year-old former Walker Cup player who divides his time between the European Tour and the PGA Tour in America. "It's a pretty nice spot where I was having some beers with friends when a local lad came up to me. He asked if I was Graeme McDowell. I said I was and wondered if he wanted an autograph.

"Then he said, 'You get it pretty laid off at the top, don't you?' I replied, 'I guess I do.' Then he said, 'Get a bit of work done on that, will you?' And I said, 'Fantastic, thanks a lot for that.' I thought I'll want to see that guy on the range on Friday morning."

The inside track about a hitch in his swing was already old news to McDowell, who had been working on improving his technique with coach Claude Harmon. Nevertheless, the observation was shrewd enough. "He knew his stuff," McDowell added. "It was something I was working on anyway. But it was a pretty funny moment."

On a subtle, testing links complicated enough to give every player in the field pause for thought, McDowell came out with a clear picture in his mind about what he wanted to achieve.

From the moment he rifled a four iron onto the par-5 fifth green and made a two-putt birdie, McDowell was off and running. He added an eight-foot birdie putt on the seventh before missing the putting surface at the short ninth and holing a sand wedge from a greenside bunker. He capitalised on that good break with another two-putt birdie on the par-5 10th. At the 11th, a short par-4, he hit wedge to 12 feet and made the 12-foot putt before rounding off with a birdie at the 16th. It was a day when McDowell took advantage of the par-5s and the game seemed ridiculously simple.

McDowell had gleaned extra knowledge about the intricacies of the links when he took advantage of missing the cut in the Barclays Scottish Open at Loch Lomond by travelling south earlier than expected to the Wirral. Well aware of how Phil Mickelson had re-written the book on preparing for major championships, he chose to put in extra work on Sunday and Monday at Royal Liverpool.

"If you look at the way Phil is preparing for majors these days, there's no doubt that extra bit of work can really pay off when you get away from the circus which leads up to major championships," McDowell said. "If you can spend time at the venue, outside the big-time atmosphere, then that can be a big help. It was to me. The 27 holes with my coach on Sunday and Monday when we were dissecting the course was invaluable. I experimented with a lot of different shots and I felt very well prepared."

Having grown up in Portrush—he thinks that experience of links golf gave him an edge over most of the field—and gone on to become the best college golfer in America, McDowell is talented enough to compete at all the majors and follow in the footsteps of another Ulsterman, Fred Daly, who became the only Irish golfer to win The Open, at Hoylake in 1947.

While setting the pace at The Open can often lead to anonymity rather than glory, Bill Longmuir twice grabbed pole positions in 1979 and 1984 but never won a regular European Tour event. McDowell sees a different future for himself. "There's no substitute for confidence and playing well on the big stage," he said. "I think I first realised I had the game to do well at this level at St Andrews in 2005 when I had a chance to win and played well enough to do it."

A season which started with a spate of missed cuts in America, McDowell learned more about the shortcomings in his game during that dismal period than he does when his swing is on song. "Golf is the easiest game in the world when you see flags in fairways," he said. "But if your golf shot is not under control, it's very tough."

On the first day of The Open, the golf shot behaved itself and life was a breeze for McDowell, who said, "It's a much nicer place to be than the doldrums."

Second Round

An Eagle Out Of The Blue

By Andy Farrell

A stroke of genius helped Tiger Woods to the top of the leaderboard, but Ernie Els and Chris DiMarco remained in pursuit with their own brilliant performances.

At 11.42 am Tiger Woods birdied the 11th hole to take the lead in The 135th Open Championship for the first time. At 12.17 pm Woods holed a four-iron shot for an eagle 2 at the 14th hole. A little over an hour later he sat in the media centre at 12 under par, an aggregate of 132, with a three-stroke lead. Was this thing over? "No," declared Woods. "I'm not sitting here with the jug. We've got 36 more holes to go. Unless there is some kind of rain storm coming in and it's cancelled after two days, we have a long way to go."

Ironically enough a storm was forecast for Saturday, but it turned out to be nothing that would delay play, let alone derail Woods on his quest for a third Open title. The only thing he underestimated at Friday lunchtime was that half the field still

Tiger Woods led on 132 with one of the day's three 65s.

had plenty more than 36 holes to play. The second round was still a long way from being completed and Ernie Els still had a contribution to make, cutting the American's halfway lead to one stroke by the end of the day.

Friday's play was one to savour, but even more so because an intriguing contest was guaranteed over the weekend. Within the space of an hour, first Chris DiMarco bettered Graeme McDowell's course record of 24 hours earlier by one stroke, then Woods matched his countryman's 65. Five hours later still, Els became the third player to register a seven-under-par round.

Each had produced a wondrous round of golf but, in the strictest terms, Els's was the best of the lot. He played in the afternoon when there was more breeze than in the morning—it was another day of generally calm weather, the greens were that bit firmer after another hot day under the sun, and he faced the prospect of having to catch a distant leader. Many others went out that afternoon with a similar purpose, but only the South African succeeded. He was the only player all day not to drop a stroke to par.

2

"Adam Scott is a major champion in waiting. The young Aussie has the tools and is getting the experience."

—**Melanie Hauser,** *PGATOUR.com*

"If Sergio Garcia's career ended today, it would be regarded as a success. But there is a concurrent element of unfinished business about Sergio. This is what happens when you are a true wonder child. You can't get away with merely being very good. It's simply understood that you must fulfil your promise."

—**Bob Ryan,** *The Boston Globe*

"South African Ernie Els looks the only player capable of keeping pace with Tiger Woods after rounds of 68 and 65 left him breathing down the World No 1's neck on 11 under."

—**David Facey,** *The Sun*

"Phil Mickelson made amends for hitting a young fan during his round by signing a glove and apologizing. The world No 2 pulled his tee shot on the 459-yard 17th into the crowd, hitting the youngster on the arm."

—**Phil Casey,** *Liverpool Daily Post*

"It seems an obvious point, but the reason I love golf tournaments is that the spectators are motivated by a very benign and sportsmanly impulse: they simply want to see every player play well; they want to see every player get the damn ball in the damn hole."

—**Lynne Truss,** *The Times*

Ernie Els posted his 65 in the afternoon to join Saturday's final pairing.

But, as ever, it was Woods who took the breath away with the drama of his assault on the leaderboard. One stroke of brilliance will always be associated with his triumph at Hoylake. It came after he had followed his usual strategy of hitting a two iron off the tee at the 14th, a hole of 456 yards. Named Hilbre after the island in the Dee estuary, the hole is similar to the 12th in that it doglegs from right to left around the sand dunes at the far end of the course.

Woods was left with a second shot of around 212 yards to the hole, but so far back was he that he could not see the flagstick for the mounds that guard the angle of the dogleg. From behind, like many of his long-iron approach shots, his swing looked a thing of beauty. Neither Woods, nor his caddie, Steve Williams, could see the result

Friday Weather

Dry and sunny with a westerly breeze, stiffening in the evening.

of his four iron. Up at the green, most of the gallery could not see him swing. Suddenly, out of the blue, a ball arrived on the green, pitching around 10 yards short of the flag, then bouncing four or five times before diving into the hole.

An instinctive, gasping roar went up from the spectators, but no one was quite sure what they had just seen, nor who had hit the shot. It might have been Tiger's policy for the week to lay back off the tee, but it was still not natural to think of Woods hitting an approach shot first in a group with Nick Faldo and Shingo Katayama.

"Who was it?" "Was it Tiger?" When confirmation came, the roars came again, but the lack of an immediate all-mighty sound had perplexed Woods back on the fairway. A brief stunned look soon cleared to delight and a high-five with Williams as they received confirmation from a television reporter that the ball had gone in the hole. As he approached the green the gallery gave him a prolonged standing ovation as usually befits the champion at the 18th on Sunday. This was just the preview.

"I had 194 yards to the front of the green," Woods explained later. "I was trying to land the ball on the front edge and let it chase on wherever it chases on. On the 12th I had 190 and hit a nice little

Chris DiMarco managed a 65 despite pars on two of the par-5 holes, while advancing to third place and trailing by three strokes.

Second Round Leaders

HOLE	1	2	3	4	5	6	7	8	9	10	11	12	13	14	15	16	17	18	TOTAL
PAR	4	4	4	4	5	3	4	4	3	5	4	4	3	4	3	5	4	5	
Tiger Woods	4	4	[5]	(3)	(4)	3	4	(3)	3	(4)	(3)	4	3	(2)	3	(4)	4	5	65-132
Ernie Els	4	4	(3)	4	(4)	(2)	4	4	3	(4)	4	4	3	(3)	3	(4)	4	(4)	65-133
Chris DiMarco	(3)	(3)	4	4	5	3	4	(3)	(2)	(4)	(3)	4	3	4	(2)	5	[5]	(4)	65-135
Retief Goosen	4	4	(3)	4	(3)	3	4	(3)	3	(4)	4	4	3	4	[4]	(3)	[5]	(4)	66-136
Miguel Angel Jimenez	(3)	4	4	(3)	(3)	3	[5]	[5]	3	5	[5]	4	3	4	3	5	4	(4)	70-137
Adam Scott	4	[5]	4	(3)	(4)	3	[5]	4	3	(4)	(3)	4	3	4	3	5	4	(4)	69-137
Mikko Ilonen	4	[6]	(3)	4	(4)	3	4	4	3	(4)	(3)	4	3	4	(2)	5	4	5	69-137
Robert Rock	4	[5]	[5]	[5]	(4)	3	4	4	3	(3)	(3)	4	3	4	(2)	5	4	(4)	69-138
Thaworn Wiratchant	4	4	(3)	4	(4)	3	4	4	3	(4)	4	[5]	3	4	3	(4)	4	(4)	68-139
Rory Sabbatini	[5]	[5]	4	4	5	3	(3)	4	3	5	(3)	(3)	(2)	4	3	(4)	[5]	5	70-139
Graeme McDowell	[5]	4	4	4	5	3	4	4	3	(4)	4	4	3	4	3	5	4	[6]	73-139
Ben Crane	4	[5]	4	[5]	(4)	3	4	(3)	3	5	[5]	4	3	4	3	(3)	4	5	71-139
G. Fernandez-Castano	4	4	4	4	5	3	4	[5]	3	(3)	4	4	3	[5]	(2)	(4)	4	(4)	69-139
Brett Rumford	4	4	[5]	(3)	(4)	3	4	4	[4]	5	4	4	3	[5]	3	(4)	4	(4)	71-139
Jerry Kelly	(3)	4	4	4	(3)	[4]	[5]	4	3	(4)	4	4	3	4	3	(3)	4	(4)	67-139
Marcus Fraser	4	[5]	4	(3)	[6]	(2)	4	4	3	5	4	4	3	[5]	3	(4)	4	(4)	71-139
Angel Cabrera	(3)	4	4	4	(4)	3	(3)	4	3	(4)	4	4	3	4	3	[6]	4	(4)	68-139
Mark Calcavecchia	4	4	(3)	4	(4)	(2)	4	[5]	3	(3)	4	[5]	[4]	(3)	(2)	[6]	4	(4)	68-139
Sergio Garcia	(3)	4	4	4	(4)	3	(3)	4	3	5	4	[5]	[4]	4	3	5	4	5	71-139
Jim Furyk	4	[5]	4	4	5	3	[5]	4	(2)	(4)	4	4	(2)	4	3	5	4	5	71-139
Robert Allenby	[5]	4	4	4	5	3	4	4	(2)	(4)	4	(3)	[4]	[5]	3	(4)	4	(4)	70-139

Graeme McDowell took bogeys on the first and final holes.

four iron up on the green and I was basically hitting the same shot, just trying to hold the ball in the wind. I really hit it flush and held it nicely. I was looking at the left of the TV tower, and if the wind blows it over, that's fine, if it doesn't, then it will be at the flag or a little left of the flag and it depends on the bounce. I was just trying to get my 4 and move on. It happened to go in.

"But we didn't know at first whether it had gone in or hit the flag and ended up right next to it. I asked one of the TV guys there and they said it went in and that's when I knew. Otherwise, I couldn't tell by the reaction because it was one of those where it could have gone in or maybe it just hit the flag and everybody was oohing and aahing."

On Friday Hilbre ranked as the hardest hole on the course, and over the week it proved the second most difficult. Golf may be a game of how many

Robert Rock was the leading British player at six under par.

Ben Crane returned a 71.

rather than how, but so often it is how Tiger does things that gets the attention of his peers. "That must have been an unbelievable shot," said Els, "because I hit a four iron myself and I thought I hit a great shot to 16 feet left of the hole and I made birdie. I thought that was my best hole of the day."

"I can't believe it," said first-round leader McDowell. "I've just watched Tiger making a 2 at a hole where he had absolutely no right to be firing at the flag." McDowell had not slept especially well with the lead—he put it down to the heat rather than nerves—but was grateful to be back out on the course early on Friday morning. At least, he was until he suffered his first bogey of the Championship at the opening hole. The magic of his opening round was not quite there and his putter was in no mood to help him out. The 26-year-old should prove something more substantial than some of the more obscure first-day Open leaders, so the experience will be invaluable.

Having scored a 73 to be five under par, McDowell was no longer the leading player from Britain or Ireland. Instead, that honour belonged not to one of the battalion of other home hopes, but to Robert Rock. A teaching professional at the Swingers Golf Centre in Warwickshire, Rock made his name with some high finishes in the Benson and Hedges International and the PGA Championship in 2003. He lost his European Tour card the following year, but won it back at the qualifying tournament for 2006.

Playing in The Open for the first time in 2005 at St Andrews was a dream come true and, like McDowell, he qualified via a seven-

> **It's a Fact**
>
> The aggregate of 132 by Tiger Woods equalled the lowest score for the first 36 holes in relation to par, 12 under par, in the history of The Open. Other 12-under aggregates for the first 36 holes were the 132s at St Andrews in 1990 by Nick Faldo and Greg Norman and the 130 at Muirfield (par-71 golf course) in 1992 by Faldo. The latter score by Faldo is considered the record for the first 36 holes.

'What's Gone Wrong With Scottish Golf?'

Paul Lawrie

Colin Montgomerie

Sandy Lyle

The home of golf's attachment to The Open is so all-consuming that the absence of even a single player among the army of challengers who made up the qualifiers for the closing two rounds at Hoylake was greeted with a mixture of dismay in Scotland and bewilderment elsewhere.

The cry of "What's gone wrong with Scottish golf?" was heard far beyond the border with England. In The Open's infancy, the tournament was so dominated by Scots that no fewer than 18 stagings of the Championship were completed before a golfer of any other nationality finished in the top four. And if the 19th century seemed like a distant mirror to examine contemporary Scottish embarrassment over the game they gifted to the rest of the world, the last European to win a major championship was Aberdeen's Paul Lawrie in 1999.

Just 12 months earlier in St Andrews, Colin Montgomerie finished runner-up to Tiger Woods while Lloyd Saltman won the Silver Medal for leading amateur from another Scot, Eric Ramsay. But at Hoylake only four Scots—Montgomerie, Paul Lawrie, Sandy Lyle, and Scott Drummond—qualified for the Championship. It was Scotland's smallest ever representation in the oldest tournament. When the doomsday scenario came to pass that not one scored well enough to make the 36-hole cut, it was a calamity without precedent since the competition was first held at Prestwick in 1860.

For much of the second round, Drummond, the former PGA champion who was born in England of Scottish parents, had been expected to fly the flag on level par. Only when a cut of one under par was confirmed on Friday evening, did the latest hammer blow to Scottish self-esteem

hit home. Drummond had teed off at 6.30 am and felt his cause wasn't helped by the hubbub which always surrounds a modern-day Open. "We had a lot of distractions," he said.

Although it was once said of Montgomerie that he could hear a sweet being unwrapped 100 yards away, he wasn't about to blame extraneous noise for a calamitous run of bogeys and a double bogey on the second nine which sent the runner-up in the US Open at Winged Foot packing from The Open at the halfway mark for the first time since 1998 at Royal Birkdale. Montgomerie played poorly and putted worse. As for Scotland's past champions, Lyle had a chance of getting through until he ran up a double-bogey 6 on the 17th hole, and Lawrie finished out of sorts on six over par.

—**Mike Aitken**

man playoff for four spots at the International Final Qualifying at Sunningdale. Rock was the last man in, after a 15-foot putt at the seventh extra hole. Another member of that lucky quartet, South African Richard Sterne, also had a memorable morning when he holed in one at the 161-yard 15th hole using a seven iron.

Rock did not have the best of starts, bogeying the second, the third, and the fourth to go back to level par. He got one shot back with a birdie at the fifth and then came home in 32, a run initiated by an eagle at the 10th, where he hit a three wood to four feet. His second nine was matched by Woods and only bettered by Charl Schwartzel and Peter Lonard, both of whom had been two over for

Players Below Par	64
Players At Par	12
Players Above Par	79

the Championship at the turn before finishing at four under.

After birdies at the 11th and the 15th, Rock's name was up on the leaderboards along with the likes of Woods and DiMarco. "I didn't see it until the 17th," said the 29-year-old. "I only had to finish in bounds at the last hole to finish okay." Another birdie gave him a second successive 69 for 138, six under par.

An early hint that the scoring would be exceptional came from Miguel Angel Jimenez. Watched by a band of fans named the "Miguels"—all having frizzy wigs and cigars—Jimenez birdied the first and the fourth and then holed a putt from 15 feet for an eagle at the fifth. At nine under par he was briefly four ahead of the field. The Spaniard would soon slide back, however, with bogeys at the seventh and eighth and finished with a 70 to be seven under. He was joined on the same mark by Adam Scott and Finland's Mikko Ilonen, who both scored 69s.

Retief Goosen edged one in front of them after a 66 which contained an outward half of 31. An eagle at the fifth as well as birdies at the third and the eighth put the South African in contention to record his fifth successive top-10 finish in The Open, but he would fade over the weekend. His front nine score was equalled by Marco Ruiz, a 31-year-old from Paraguay and a nephew of Vicente Fernandez, who was playing in his second Open and who had only 23 putts in a second round of 70, and DiMarco.

Then leading by four, Miguel Angel Jimenez saved par here at the sixth hole.

Excerpts FROM THE Press

"Colin Montgomerie threw away five shots in just four holes to crash out of The Open after two days at the head of the line of top British golfers who missed the cut."

—**Matthew Dunn,** *Daily Express*

"When does a golf shot have the effect of the dive of a hawk or the turn of a great thoroughbred's hoof or a punch delivered by Muhammad Ali? If we didn't know before, we knew in a moment that stretched credibility to another high noon of burning heat yesterday. It is when it is made by Tiger Woods."

—**James Lawton,** *The Independent*

"Chris DiMarco smashed the Hoylake course record to tug at The Tiger's heels. And then he revealed his dead mother Norma was looking down, willing him on."

—**Dave Armitage,** *Daily Star*

"Graeme McDowell tossed and turned all Thursday night but insisted this was only due to the heat in his bedroom. Yet the Portrush hot-shot admitted he had butterflies on the first tee and fluttering nerves played a part in his bogey at that hole as he hooked his opening shot into scutch and left his next in a greenside bunker."

—**Karl MacGinty,** *Irish Independent*

"David Duval is getting closer. With each round and tournament, he zeroes in a little more on the kind of form that once made him No 1."

—**Vartan Kupelian,** *Detroit News*

In the Words of the Competitors...

❝

"When you come over here to play, you know the golf course is always going to be fair, and it's just a matter of the weather."

—Tiger Woods

"I would like to see more of these courses in the States, I really would. It's so much fun to play."

—Chris DiMarco

"All things considered, the round could have gone pretty badly, but I managed to turn it around. So I'm pretty happy to be where I am."

—Rory Sabbatini

"The front nine has been good to me, nine under par so far. It's on the back nine that I am struggling."

—Retief Goosen

"It would be great to walk down No 18 on Sunday afternoon and receive the Silver Medal. But there's still 36 holes to play. There's a lot of golf left."

—amateur Marius Thorp

"I was nine under par and then made three bogeys, so that was disappointing. So seven under is not as good as nine or 10, but not to worry."

—Miguel Angel Jimenez

❞

Retief Goosen returned a 66 and went out in 31, with four birdies.

Despite losing in two playoffs for major championships, DiMarco had missed the cut in four of the last five. His 2006 season never got going, although it began well with victory in Abu Dhabi, his first win for four years. In March he had a skiing accident and injured his back and ribs. Having finally got over the injury, his mother, Norma, died suddenly at the beginning of July.

"I have a great peace about me this week. I never considered not playing The Open," DiMarco said. "My mom was a huge supporter of me and she would be angry if I didn't play. My dad, Rich, is here watching. It is therapeutic for me to be inside the ropes playing, and it is therapeutic for him to be outside the ropes watching."

When he got to Hoylake, DiMarco liked what he saw. "This is golf," he said. "It's not just grip it and rip it as we have in the States all the time. When the fairways are this hard it doesn't favour the bombers because the ball runs into trouble. I wish we played more of it." As he struggled with his form while returning from injury, DiMarco tried all sorts of new putters and tinkered with his set-up. But the man who made the "claw" grip famous returned to his usual putter and style the previous week. "I went back to what I did and stopped thinking so much," he said.

It seemed to work as he holed acres of putts across the scorched

Reverting to his old putter, Chris DiMarco holed four putts of 20 feet or more for birdies.

greens. He made 20-footers at both the first and the second. A six iron to eight feet at the eighth produced a third birdie and the first of four in a row. He holed from 30 feet at the short ninth, then two-putted for a 4 at the 10th, and made a five-footer at the 11th. On the 15th he holed from 25 feet, before his only bogey came at the 17th. His drive had finished close to a bunker on the left of the fairway and he almost toppled in while playing his second.

An up-and-down from 60 yards at the last gave DiMarco his eighth birdie and a total of nine under par. He had topped the leaderboard for a significant part of his round, but then along came Woods. The world No 1 was only twice in the rough during his round. The first time was on the third hole, when his tee shot ran through the fairway. His second came up 20 yards short of the green from where he putted onto the green but took two more putts for his only bogey of the round. The only other time he was off the short grass was after his three-wood tee shot at the 18th, which led to him laying up and settling for a par 5.

In between times Woods produced the most staggering exhibition.

Rory Sabbatini recovered nicely.

Mark Calcavecchia and his wife/caddie, Brenda, were all smiles with his 68 to tie for ninth place at five under par.

Thailand's Thaworn Wiratchant climbed into the top 10 on 139.

He immediately picked up the shot he dropped at the third with a birdie at the fourth, where he holed from 20 feet. At the next he chipped using a four iron to a foot and made his 4 at the par-5. On the eighth green he hit a wonderful putt, from 60 feet away, but it was something of a bonus that the ball fell into the hole. Had it not, it would have been another simple tap-in.

Out in 33 strokes, Tiger then knocked his four iron onto the green at the 10th and two-putted for a birdie 4. At the 11th his approach with a wedge was delightful, somehow stopping the ball despite an initial bounce on a downslope, and naturally he holed the 12-footer for birdie. This was the moment he took the lead for the first time, but there was still the eagle at the 14th to come and an up-and-down at the 16th for a sixth birdie.

"I really felt I controlled my flight," Woods said. "I felt I was able to shape the ball both ways and control my traj"—he meant trajectory—"and keep the ball on the flight I wanted, sometimes higher,

Spectators at The Open Championship might choose from a broad selection of food and beverages.

Programmes and radios could be purchased, and the Official Merchandise Pavilion offered clothing and other items.

Round of the Day

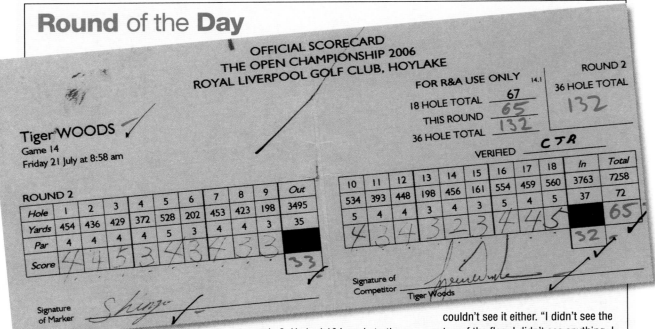

OFFICIAL SCORECARD
THE OPEN CHAMPIONSHIP 2006
ROYAL LIVERPOOL GOLF CLUB, HOYLAKE

FOR R&A USE ONLY 14.1

ROUND 2
36 HOLE TOTAL
132

18 HOLE TOTAL _67_
THIS ROUND _65_
36 HOLE TOTAL _132_

VERIFIED _CJR_

Tiger WOODS ✓
Game 14
Friday 21 July at 8:58 am

ROUND 2

Hole	1	2	3	4	5	6	7	8	9	Out	10	11	12	13	14	15	16	17	18	In	Total
Yards	454	436	429	372	528	202	453	423	198	3495	534	393	448	198	456	161	554	459	560	3763	7258
Par	4	4	4	4	5	3	4	4	3	35	5	4	4	3	4	3	5	4	5	37	72
Score	4	4	5	3	4	3	4	3	3	33	4	3	4	3	2	3	4	4	5	32	65

Signature of Marker _Shingo_

Signature of Competitor _Tiger Woods_

With one of the day's three scores of 65, seven under par, Tiger Woods posted a total in the 60s for the 16th time in 46 career rounds in The Open Championship, which includes his 66 in 1996 to equal the lowest round ever by an amateur.

The key was Woods's play with his irons, and the highlight was his four-iron shot on the par-4, 456-yard 14th hole, which went in the cup for an eagle 2. He had 194 yards to the front of the green. "I was trying to lay the ball on the front edge and let it chase on. On 12 I had 190 (yards) and hit a nice little four iron on the green, and I was basically hitting the same shot, just trying to hold the ball in the wind."

The cheering was not as great as it might have been because the spectators couldn't see and didn't know when the golf ball was coming or from whom, and obviously the players couldn't see it either. "I didn't see the top of the flag. I didn't see anything. I was too far back," Woods said.

He took a bogey 4 on the third hole, missing a six-foot putt. His six birdies were at No 4 on a nine-iron shot and a putt from 20 feet, at No 5 with a four-iron chip and a putt from 12 feet, at No 8 on a putt from 60 feet, at the par-5 No 10 on a four-iron shot and two putts from 40 feet, at No 11 with a pitching wedge and a putt from 12 feet, and at No 16 with a chip and a putt from four feet.

Low Scores

Low First Nine
Chris DiMarco	31
Retief Goosen	31
Marco Ruiz	31

Low Second Nine
Charl Schwartzel	31
Peter Lonard	31

Low Round
Ernie Els	65
Chris DiMarco	65
Tiger Woods	65

sometimes lower. If you look at most of my shots, they were around pin-high. It's awfully nice to be able to do that on a links golf course. It's not easy to do that on a links. It's easy to do when it's plugging up there. But when you have to control the bounce on the greens and fairways, yeah, I felt like I was in control of my flight today."

His total of 132 for 36 holes was two strokes outside the record set by Faldo at Muirfield in 1992, but his 12-under mark did equal the record in relation to par set by Faldo and Greg Norman at St Andrews in 1990 and matched by Faldo at Muirfield two years later. More chillingly for the field, it was the seventh time Woods had

Woods happily displayed his eagle-2 ball at the 14th hole.

Nick Faldo was an amiable playing companion.

Jerry Kelly scored birdies on Nos 16 and 18 for a 68.

An 8 on the 18th knocked John Daly out of The Open.

taken the 36-hole lead in a major championship and he had won all of the previous six times.

At least the relations between Woods and Faldo, so cold a couple of days earlier, had thawed in the heat and the brilliance of the American's display. They left the 18th green with smiles, as befitting a three-time Open champion and a player about to become a three-time Open champion. Faldo, who made some early birdies in a 71 but missed the cut, put his arm around Tiger's shoulders and asked if Matthew, his son who was also acting as his caddie, could have his driver because Tiger did not seem to need it.

"I saw the score," Els said of the Tiger-topping leaderboard when he teed off. "Obviously he's a great player, but if he's at 12 under, I thought there must be some birdies to be made out there. I felt I had to get my share of them. I felt good in the warm-up and I didn't feel the urge of pushing too much too soon or trying to hit the perfect shot. The mindset before is always to play a solid round. I didn't think I was going to shoot 65, but I needed something in the 60s. So I wasn't trying to be crazy aggressive,

Sergio Garcia missed a birdie putt on No 10, then took bogeys on Nos 12 and 13.

Angel Cabrera's 68 included 32 on the outward nine holes.

In the Words *of the* Competitors...

"It was different in the afternoon than in the morning. The greens weren't holding so well as this morning. There was a lot more wind out there. A lot of holes this morning weren't playing as difficult as they were in the afternoon."

—Sergio Garcia

"If you are playing well and you can take advantage of the par-5s, there's a chance you can shoot seven or eight under. If you don't the whole day is going to be a battle."

—Adam Scott

"I hit most every fairway, most every green, and just didn't get the putts to fall. Probably four or five putts had a good chance to go in but didn't."

—David Duval

"It's disappointing the way I am playing. I'm glad I'm here on the weekend, but I'm going to have to change something to get the golf swing to work better than it has."

—Tom Watson

The Open Is Therapeutic For DiMarco's Family
'These days have been very good for us,' Chris says

Chris DiMarco's 65 was welcome news for a number of people, first and foremost DiMarco himself, who was competing for the first time since his mother had died suddenly on the 4th of July. Norma DiMarco was, by Chris's account, an inspirational person who provided him with some of his competitiveness. Rich DiMarco was as pleased with his son's seven-under-par round as Chris was himself.

Tom Lehman would have been encouraged too at the return to form of a man best described as the heartbeat of any team of which he's a member. DiMarco had been a star of the US team in the previous autumn's Presidents Cup and to say he likes the Ryder Cup is an understatement. Unusual for an American, he regards playing in it as a greater honour than winning a major championship. But a skiing injury in the spring after he had won a tournament in the Middle East on the European Tour, a loss of form when he tried to return to competitive play before he had fully recovered, and the sudden death of his mother had combined to keep him some way from the top 10 in the US team's standings.

DiMarco's 65 added lustre to the course, too. It proved that firm and fast-running as Hoylake was, the combination of skill and guile rather than sheer length could suppress it. He used a lot of one and two irons from the tees. "I love it," DiMarco said. "It's such an equaliser because it doesn't favour the bombers." Last but not least it put DiMarco back in contention for another major championship, gave him another chance to do better than he had at the USPGA in 2004 and the Masters in 2005 when he was beaten in playoffs.

He birdied the first two holes of his outward and inward nine holes and the last two holes of the outward nine holes as well. The other two birdies of his haul of eight came at the 15th and the 18th. "Putting was the key today," DiMarco said.

"I made some good 25- to 30-footers." He certainly did. Those on the first, second, ninth, and 15th were all in that range. His putt on the eighth was eight feet, much the same length as his putt on the 18th and a few feet longer than his putt on the 11th.

DiMarco's first round, a 70, had been a typical round, also full of good putting. But this was the round that made everyone sit up and pay attention to the feisty American. DiMarco's run of lacklustre play was over. He had found an inner peace after his mother's death. Bringing his father and son, Cristian, to Hoylake with him helped them with their grieving. "Walking inside the ropes is therapeutic for me and walking outside the ropes watching me play well is therapeutic for them," DiMarco said on Friday. "These past two days have been very good for us."

—**John Hopkins**

Rich DiMarco and his grandson, Cristian, joined son Chris for The Open.

Adam Scott, at seven under par, led The Open's 23-man Australian group.

but I needed to try and get close to him. We all know what a good frontrunner he is."

Els was at four under on the first tee and at the third hit a superb seven iron to two feet for the first of seven birdies. A delicate chip along a ridge in the green gave him a six-foot birdie putt at the fifth, and he holed from 18 feet on the sixth to be three under for the round. From there it was a case of taking advantage of the par-5s. He got up and down from a bunker at the 10th for a 4, and two-putted at both the 16th and the 18th holes, as well as making a 3 at the 14th.

What Els managed, in getting to 11 under and a first weekend final group meeting with Woods since the 2000 US Open, no one else managed. Sergio Garcia was going along nicely at three under on the first nine, but again could not birdie the 10th. This time he was bunkered in two, hit a fine recovery but saw it trickle past the hole and then off the green on the other side. His chip from there lipped out. The Spaniard shot a 71 to join the group on five under, as did Jim Furyk, whose adventures included putting out of a bunker

Excerpts FROM THE Press

"Andrew Buckle, from Australia, was the last man in the field—replacing Trevor Immelman, who went home for the birth of his first child. He had to dash from America in time to tee off on Thursday. He starts the third round on a healthy three under par, but it has not all gone smoothly; his regular caddie, Andrew Murphy, is still in Missouri. Neither man had enough credit on their plastic for two flights."

—Claire Middleton, *The Daily Telegraph*

"At first glance, the immediate and understandable temptation is to concede a third Open Championship and 11th major title to Tiger Woods, a player who has never lost a halfway lead in a major championship. But it is the one that is meeting some notable resistance."

—John Huggan, *The Guardian*

"BBC television's uninterrupted coverage of The Open has been outstanding and it would be discourteous not to acclaim the recruitment to its commentary team of the Australian Wayne Grady. He has words and wit, a pleasant discursive style, and thankfully does not drive us to near narcolepsy with protracted analyses of swings and putting styles."

—Ian Wooldridge, *Daily Mail*

"Tom Watson complained about his creaking joints, but still made the cut at two under. The five-times Open champion showed he can hack it with the best."

—Phil Pringle, *Saturday Sport*

at the fourth. Englishmen Greg Owen and Anthony Wall both had 73s to be four under, Owen after a drive at the last which finished a foot out of bounds and cost him a double bogey.

Also at four under was Phil Mickelson. Like Els, he had been hoping to vault himself into contention, but the left-hander did not appear to get the balance right between pressing and letting the game flow. There were only three birdies, two of them at the par-5s, in a 71. "I wanted to be patient, but obviously I'm not excited to be eight shots back," Mickelson said. "I still feel a good round tomorrow will give me a chance."

Luke Donald, after a 68, and Paul Casey, with a 70 on his 29th birthday, were also still alive on two under, but for many more there would be no tomorrow. The cut was confirmed at one under par—the lowest since 1990 at St Andrews—when

England's Andrew Marshall birdied the last hole in the third-to-last group of the day. Among those missing from weekend action would be Paul McGinley, after finishing at level par, John Daly, after hitting two balls out of bounds in an 8 at the 18th, Tom Lehman, Vijay Singh, following a second round of 76, Nick Dougherty, who grew up in Liverpool, Padraig Harrington, David Howell, Paul Lawrie, Darren Clarke, and Ian Poulter.

Nor would Colin Montgomerie be challenging at this Open. The 2005 runner-up got back to one under for the Championship at the 10th, but three bogeys and a double bogey from the 13th ended his hopes. Before teeing off he had spoken on the phone to his 13-year-old daughter Olivia, who noted, not all together encouragingly: "Daddy, Tiger's running away with this." A reasonable assessment at the time, but Woods was not clear away yet.

Round Two Hole Summary

HOLE	PAR	YARDS	EAGLES	BIRDIES	PARS	BOGEYS	D.BOGEYS	HIGHER	RANK	AVERAGE
1	4	454	0	13	97	40	5	1	4	4.26
2	4	436	0	12	88	52	3	1	2	4.31
3	4	429	0	19	98	31	4	4	6	4.22
4	4	372	0	17	112	25	2	0	10	4.08
5	5	528	9	72	60	12	3	0	17	4.54
6	3	202	0	14	111	27	4	0	9	3.14
7	4	453	0	14	98	37	5	2	4	4.26
8	4	423	0	17	117	21	0	0	12	4.03
9	3	198	0	16	116	21	2	0	11	3.06
OUT	35	3495	9	194	897	266	28	8		35.88
10	5	534	5	74	66	7	3	0	16	4.54
11	4	393	0	27	98	29	1	0	12	4.03
12	4	448	0	10	98	40	6	1	3	4.29
13	3	198	0	11	112	28	4	0	8	3.16
14	4	456	1	9	96	39	9	1	1	4.32
15	3	161	1	30	108	15	1	0	14	2.90
16	5	554	6	83	51	15	0	0	18	4.48
17	4	459	0	10	110	30	4	1	7	4.20
18	5	560	3	69	66	12	2	3	15	4.68
IN	37	3763	16	323	805	215	30	6		36.60
TOTAL	72	7258	25	517	1702	481	58	14		72.48

Tiger Woods: Playing A Links As His Father Taught Him

By David Davies

Tiger Woods had a strong suspicion that he was going to enjoy his Hoylake experience right from the moment he set eyes on the burned-brown expanse of grass that comprised this year's version of the Royal Liverpool Golf Club. "It's hard," he said, "and it's definitely fast. It's going to be a fantastic challenge this week. We don't get a chance to do this very often, but when we do, it sure brings shotmaking and creativity back into the game."

There is nothing Woods likes better than just such a challenge, offering him the chance to display the full, and incredible, range of his talents. Hoylake was not, as Colin Montgomerie was to remark, the typical American course where "you hit the ball 157.6 yards and it spins back 3.2 feet."

No, Hoylake was in near-perfect condition for a links hosting an Open, a partial drought beforehand had dried it out and some of the hottest weather the United Kingdom had ever experienced in the days immediately prior to the Championship had baked it hard. "In these conditions," Woods said, "you have to be able to control your golf ball in the air, you have to control your spin. It's not like you can go out there and hit a marginal shot and expect it to be okay. You come in with the wrong spin and you're going to pay a consequence for that."

Of course, there is a consequence of good shots as well as marginal ones, and consequently Woods produced rounds of 67 and 65 to lead after 36 holes—a position from which he has never been dislodged in a major championship.

It was a hugely impressive effort, especially given that Woods had played only six rounds of competitive golf since his father, Earl, died on 3 May, missing the cut in the US Open before finishing second in the Cialis Western Open.

In fact it was Earl who inculcated into his son his love of a challenge in general, and of that offered by links golf in particular. "He absolutely loved it when I played in the Scottish Open at Carnoustie (as an amateur in 1995), because he thought it was one of the very few times that I was able to use my imagination and create shots. In links golf you have to do that because there are so many different options. He thoroughly enjoyed it, watching me shape shots, hitting all sorts of weird shots—he got a big kick out of that."

Even if Earl is gone, his legacy lives on. "There's not a day that I'll go through in life without thinking about my dad," he said. "The bond we had, I think it transcended the normal parent-child relationship, which is probably why I think about him more when

I'm out playing and practising. The fundamentals, all the fundamentals that I learned were from him.

"Anytime I go back to basics and work on grip, posture, and stance, all the things I learned from him, I think of him."

Woods, though, has come to terms with his loss. "He's not here any more," he said. "It's not like I can pick up the phone and say 'Pops, what do you think about my putting stroke?' Those days aren't here any more, but I have so many wonderful memories that I'll look back on it with smiles every time."

There were rather more smiles than usual during the first two rounds from the more usually poker-faced Woods. The smile on the 18th hole after an eagle putt had fallen to take him to five under par was probably one of relief that a good round had got a decent reward, but the grin he gave at the 14th hole in the second round was one of sheer delight.

Playing well, but by no means sensationally, he was four under par after 13 holes and hit a two iron off the tee down the middle, leaving him 194 yards to the front of the green. "I was just trying to land the ball on the front edge with a four iron," Woods said, "and let it chase on in there and get my par 4 and go. It happened to go in."

The shot, to an elevated green, was blind to Woods, but the cheers told him the ball had gone in and he high-fived Steve Williams, his caddie. Then, as he had obviously given his boss the right advice as to the correct club, Williams playfully suggested a change of roles, offering the bag to Woods.

It was light-heartedly declined, which was just as well for the spectators who were witnessing some wonderful iron play. Woods was asked afterwards about his striking of the mid and long irons and said, "I felt like I was able to hit the golf ball on the flight I really wanted to."

He was asked had he ever done it better? "Yes," he said, "I think I did a pretty good job at Pebble Beach in 2000." That, of course, was the US Open which, perhaps ominously, he won by a mere 15 strokes.

Caddie Steve Williams celebrated with Woods when the eagle-2 was confirmed.

Third Round

It's Another Tiger Hunt

By Andy Farrell

Sergio Garcia joined the chasing pack, but Tiger Woods kept himself in front despite some uncharacteristic putting lapses on the inward nine.

Tiger Woods did not run away with The 135th Open Championship on the third day, either. Nor was the alternative prospect of a "Duel in the Sun" reprise—for Tom Watson and Jack Nicklaus at Turnberry in 1977 read Woods and Ernie Els at Hoylake—fully realised. It was all far more interesting than that. Here was the ideal Saturday at a major championship, the field scrambling to set up a intriguing Sunday.

There were more fine scores to be had in the third round, but not for Woods or Els. Both scored 71s to allow plenty of other challengers to stake a claim. Chief among them was Sergio Garcia, who equalled the course record with the fourth 65 of the week. The young Spaniard jumped from five

A leaping Sergio Garcia viewed his approach to the 11th.

under par to 12 under par and only a birdie at the 18th saw Woods preserve his one-stroke lead from the night before.

Of course, whenever Tiger gets in front, the numbers suggest he goes on to win. This was the 11th time in major championships that he had held the lead after 54 holes, or at least a share of it, and the world No 1 had proved victorious on all of the previous 10. But unlike on some previous occasions, the twin threat of a magnificent golf course and a pack of pursuers was not allowing Tiger to romp away.

It might have been different, however, if he had not done something very un-Tiger-like on the inward nine of the third round. Woods three-putted, not once, not twice, but three times. Asked if he was surprised not to have been further ahead, Woods replied, "If I would have just putted normally, I would have. I thought I hit the ball great today. Just take away my three-putts, three of them in eight holes, I would have a four-shot lead.

"These were some of the most difficult pins I've ever seen in The Open Championship," Tiger added. "It was a challenge to get the ball close. I really

Ernie Els was not at his best off the tees but returned a 71 thanks to his short game.

It's a
Fact

Sergio Garcia's 29 on the first nine of the third round was the 12th score under 30 for nine holes in the history of The Open. The record of 28 was set by Denis Durnian on the first nine at Royal Birkdale in 1983. Including Garcia, 11 players have returned 29 for nine holes, starting with Peter Thomson and Tom Haliburton on the first nine at Royal Lytham in 1958.

had to hit some quality shots. But on the greens you really had to watch your pace because every green is a slightly different speed."

By contrast, Els was ragged from tee to green and it was only his short game that kept him in contention. With Woods at 13 under, Els shared second place with Garcia and Chris DiMarco, who returned a 69. Jim Furyk and Angel Cabrera both scored 66s to be two behind Woods, with Japan's Hideto Tanihara a further shot back after also taking Route 66. Only Els and DiMarco had been within three strokes of Woods the previous evening.

"Stats don't lie," DiMarco said as he reviewed Tiger's place at the top of the leaderboard. "Obviously, he's a pretty good frontrunner and usually he's got a five- or six-shot lead. Tomorrow he has a one-shot lead. But the guy has a knack for winning, so it's going to be tough to beat him."

Still, Saturday's play proved once again that golf can be as unpredictable as the weather. A thunderstorm was forecast on the Wirral

Chris DiMarco posted a 69 with four birdies on the last nine.

Saturday Weather

Sunny start becoming cloudy later, with a variable breeze.

"Hoylake has taken a bit of a beating from low scorers but has produced a sterling list of leaders. The combination of difficulty and scoreability has quickly earned it a Masters-like reputation for separating the top players of varying styles and giving them a chance to make something happen."

—Scott Michaux,
The Augusta Chronicle

"Every year we buy into The Open dream. We plonk our money on a Brit and when the bookies have paid out all we have is a pocket bulging with ifs, buts and maybes."

—James Mossop,
The Sunday Telegraph

"The fickle finger of fate poked Lee Westwood in his Open eye from all angles. One of the last big-name Brits left at Royal Liverpool was buzzed on the first by a helicopter zooming overhead as starter Ivor Robson introduced him on the tee. And that wasn't the end of it."

—Steve Millar, *Daily Star Sunday*

"The putts that stubbornly refused to drop during the first two rounds of The Open Championship finally relented. And with each birdie putt that fell into the cup, Scott Verplank inched closer to the top 10 places on the leaderboard—and those all-important Ryder Cup points that would come with such a finish."

—Helen Ross, PGATOUR.com

Despite bogeys on the 12th and 14th, Jim Furyk finished in 66, tied for fifth.

for the afternoon and the tee times were moved up by an hour. But though it got humid and clammy, and the clouds became darkly threatening, and the breeze switched around, the storm did not come and play was uninterrupted. Instead, the only growing storm was created by the two-ball of Garcia and Furyk.

Their best ball would have been 12 under par, but it helped when Garcia holed his second shot, with a nine iron, at the second hole for an eagle 2. "I hit a very nice tee shot with my five wood," Garcia explained, "and then I had 167 yards to the hole. The wind was just off to the left, maybe a touch of help, but not much. I cut a nice solid nine iron in there. As soon as it came out it looked really good. I was hoping for it to be the right distance and then I'd have a kick-in birdie. It is always nice when you see it go in like that."

Garcia can hit some sublime iron shots but sometimes has trouble on the greens, or "rolling the potato," as he puts it. But not here, obviously. There must have been something about the hole location, as a few minutes later Thaworn Wiratchant also holed his approach shot at the second, but unfortunately for the Thai he went on to post a 74. Garcia, however, took full advantage and also pulled Furyk along in his slipstream. The American might have lost the hole had it been match play, but he rolled in a 20-footer for birdie to get his own round going.

Garcia had to save par at the fourth when his second finished under the face of a bunker, but a beautiful recovery put him only a foot away. Both Garcia and Furyk found the green at the fifth in two strokes and two-putted for birdies. Furyk, the

Tiger Woods had three three-putt greens.

Third Round Leaders

HOLE	1	2	3	4	5	6	7	8	9	10	11	12	13	14	15	16	17	18	
PAR	4	4	4	4	5	3	4	4	3	5	4	4	3	4	3	5	4	5	TOTAL
Tiger Woods	4	[5]	4	4	(4)	(2)	[5]	4	3	5	(3)	4	3	[5]	3	(4)	[5]	(4)	71-203
Sergio Garcia	4	(2)	4	4	(4)	3	(3)	(3)	(2)	5	4	4	3	4	3	5	4	(4)	65-204
Chris DiMarco	4	4	(3)	4	5	3	[5]	4	[4]	5	(3)	(3)	(2)	4	3	(4)	4	5	69-204
Ernie Els	[5]	(3)	4	4	5	3	[5]	4	(2)	5	4	4	[4]	4	3	(4)	4	(4)	71-204
Jim Furyk	4	(3)	4	4	(4)	(2)	(3)	4	3	(4)	(3)	[5]	3	[5]	3	(4)	(3)	5	66-205
Angel Cabrera	[5]	4	4	(3)	(4)	3	4	4	3	(4)	4	(3)	[4]	(3)	(2)	(3)	4	5	66-205
Hideto Tanihara	4	4	4	4	(4)	(2)	[5]	(3)	3	(4)	4	4	3	4	(2)	(4)	4	(4)	66-206
Mark Calcavecchia	(3)	4	4	(3)	(4)	3	[5]	4	3	(4)	(3)	[5]	3	4	(2)	5	[5]	(4)	68-207
Adam Scott	4	[5]	4	[5]	(4)	3	(3)	4	3	(4)	4	4	3	4	3	(4)	4	5	70-207
Andres Romero	4	4	[5]	(3)	(4)	3	(3)	4	3	(4)	(3)	[5]	3	(3)	3	5	4	5	68-208
Greg Owen	4	[5]	4	(3)	(4)	3	4	4	3	(4)	(3)	4	3	[5]	3	(4)	4	(4)	68-208
Peter Lonard	(3)	[5]	(3)	4	5	3	4	(3)	3	(4)	4	4	3	4	3	(4)	4	5	68-208
Robert Allenby	[5]	[5]	4	(3)	5	(2)	4	4	3	(4)	4	4	(2)	4	3	5	4	(4)	69-208
Jerry Kelly	4	4	4	(3)	5	[4]	(3)	4	3	(4)	4	4	3	4	3	(4)	[5]	(4)	69-208
Retief Goosen	4	4	(3)	[5]	[6]	[4]	(3)	4	3	(4)	4	[5]	3	(3)	3	5	[5]	(4)	72-208

The figures for the early starters were just being posted on Saturday morning on the main scoreboard.

Meanwhile, the Claret Jug was on display.

US Open champion in 2003, then holed from 15 feet at the sixth and 40 feet at the seventh to set up an outward half of 31.

But Garcia was only just reaching his dazzling peak. At both the seventh and the eighth the 26-year-old hit approach shots with his wedge that finished six feet away, and then at the 198-yard ninth he struck an eight iron to three feet. The three birdies to complete the first nine meant an outward sequence of 29 strokes. It was the 11th time nine holes in The Open had been covered in as few shots and left him only one behind the record holder, Denis Durnian, who shot a 28 on the first nine at Royal Birkdale in 1983.

"We had an exciting first nine," Furyk said. "Sergio hit some beautiful irons. You can feed off seeing good shots and I felt really in control of my game." The American birded the first two holes on

A Shot Worthy Of A Roar

Garcia's eagle-2 at the second excites the crowd

Just once in the storied history of the old Championship has anyone covered nine holes in fewer strokes. When Sergio Garcia raced to the turn in 29 flawless shots in the third round, only Denis Durnian's 28 over the outward half at Royal Birkdale in 1983 stood apart.

Ernie Els, Peter Thomson, Tony Jacklin, and Ian Baker-Finch are the past champions among the 10 players who have matched Garcia's formidable scoring at previous Championships. None of those great players, though, struck the ball with greater authority than the Spaniard did at Royal Liverpool or prompted a more emotional response from the crowds who deserted Anfield for Hoylake.

Accustomed to cheering on Luis Garcia and Xabi Alonso, two of Spain's finest footballers, in the red and white of Liverpool FC, many of the 45,500 scousers who flocked to watch the first Open held on the Wirral in four decades greeted Sergio's holed nine iron at the second hole with a roar worthy of the Kop.

When that shot from 167 yards bounced into the hole—he had already made a terrific par save on the first—Garcia was so uplifted by the acclaim that for the first time in many moons he was transformed into the young master of the links who won the Amateur at Muirfield and promised to

transform the profile of European golf as no one else has done since the incomparable Seve Ballesteros.

"Holing out at the second gave me great momentum," Garcia recalled. "I was able to relax then. I felt pretty good going out in 29. I was controlling my trajectory and hit a lot of nice shots. On the second, I'd hit five wood off the tee. The wind was off to the left, maybe a touch of help, but not much. I just cut a good, solid nine iron."

In search of Ryder Cup points as well as his first major championship, Garcia had returned to Britain the previous week at Loch Lomond to play in the Barclays Scottish Open for the first time in six years. The competition was helpful to his game and the Spaniard travelled to Hoylake knowing he only needed to improve a little. As it turned out, he improved a lot.

Playing with Garcia and drawing enough inspiration to card an impressive 66 of his own, Jim Furyk savoured a close-up view of the Spaniard's imperious ball-striking on a shot-maker's course peppered with pot bunkers to punish errant blows.

"It was just a joy to watch someone play his iron shots so beautifully," said the American Ryder Cup player. "When you are playing with someone who is hitting really good shots—Sergio hit it inside six or seven feet on three successive holes

Garcia went out in 29.

toward the turn—it lifts everyone. You could feed off them."

On the inward half, some of the fizz went out of Garcia's play, though there was a peerless wedge shot from the rough on the 11th which drew gasps of admiration from the gallery. He only found one more birdie on the last hole for 65 and 12 under par, which was good enough to get into the last group on Sunday with Tiger Woods.

—**Mike Aitken**

the second nine, making a 15-footer at the 11th, and at 11 under par was briefly tied for the lead with Garcia, Woods, and Els. Garcia's first two rounds had stalled after the turn for home and the same happened again.

For the third day running Garcia parred the par-5 10th, and then at the 11th, following a spectacular wedge shot from the rough on a bank to the left of the fairway, he missed a birdie chance from three feet. Garcia got stuck in par mode, but Furyk missed the greens at the 12th and the 14th and dropped a shot each time. He got them back at the 16th and the 17th, where he holed from 25 feet, and settled for a 66.

Furyk finished fourth in The Open in both 1997 and 1998, but had

A second 68 placed Mark Calcaveccia in a tie for eighth.

Scott Verplank was disappointed with his 5-5 finish.

Low Scores

Low First Nine	
Sergio Garcia	29
Low Second Nine	
Angel Cabrera	32
Low Round	
Sergio Garcia	65

not made a cut since 2000. He put the pattern down to improving his game to hit the ball higher in the United States. "I was known as a good wind player and hit the ball flat and low," he said. "But to compete on the newer courses in the game I changed equipment and adapted my game. What I've done a poor job on at the last few Opens is adapting back to the bump-and-run style, but I'm finally seeing the results."

Garcia did have one more birdie in him and it came at the last, where he lagged a putt from short of the green and tapped in for his 4. He would be the only player all day not to make a bogey. "I was very pleased with the way I hit the ball all day, even though I managed to make only one birdie on the second nine," he said. It was his lowest round in a major championship, but in order to win his first major title—something many thought would have occurred by now—another 18 holes awaited. "I just want to do the same things as today, commit to every shot and enjoy it as much as possible. Today was a thrill with the people and all the cheers on to the greens."

It was a feature of the day that none of the later starters enjoyed a

With his 66, Angel Cabrera was flying high.

In the Words of the Competitors...

"These are some of the most difficult pins that I've ever seen in The Open Championship, and it was a good challenge trying to get the ball close."

—Tiger Woods

"Any time you are in position to win a major, and you experience the pressure that goes with it, you have something to draw from. And I certainly have some good memories. I know one thing is that you've got to play your game."

—Chris DiMarco

"There are not too many of us 46-year-olds competing at this level. The fact that I'm still competing in The Open at 46 is good news for me."

—Mark Calcavecchia

"I love playing over here as it examines your whole game. You have to hit high shots, low shots, curve it into the wind, curve it with the wind."

—Scott Verplank

really low round. From the last seven pairings, only DiMarco broke 70 and the only other players under par were Ben Crane and Adam Scott, plus Woods and Els. Early in the day it was a different matter. Andrew Marshall, having only just made the cut with a birdie at the 18th approaching 9 pm on Friday, found himself as the first player out on Saturday morning. He played on his own, rejecting a playing marker, as he had done in the European Open two weeks before. The Norfolk man enjoyed his solitary round and a 68 took him from a tie for 57th place to a tie for 25th.

Els Finds A Way To Score

By Lewine Mair

Ernie Els said it was 'fiendishly difficult' to have back-to-back low scores.

Nick Hastings, one of the leading psychologists on the European Tour, approved Ernie Els's approach as he set out to play alongside Tiger Woods in the last pairing of the third day. Some months earlier, when Els and Woods were tied after 72 holes of the Dubai Desert Classic and had to return to the 18th tee for the playoff, Hastings had taken note as Woods initiated the kind of firm handshake which, according to the mind men, "makes a statement." In Dubai, Woods proceeded to drive down the middle and Els hit into the trees.

At Hoylake, starting out one shot behind Woods, Els was the initiator of the handshake. After that, and a strapping tee shot to go with it, Els hit a wedge into a greenside bunker and failed to get up and down. Woods made a mistake at the second when he, too, hit into sand. At that, people sensed that they were about to see as much fight as flair over the afternoon.

At the seventh, their stumbling coincided. Els smashed his tee shot into a gorse bush and was forced to take a drop. His third took a dive into a pot bunker from which he salvaged a bogey. Woods, meantime, had hit into a bunker by the green and scored a bogey of his own.

Both were out in level-par 35 and back in a one-under 36 for relatively mundane 71s which left Woods's one-shot lead in the Championship intact. "You're not always going to have your best stuff," Els said, "and you have to find a way of scoring. That's what I did today." Woods, in a reference to how they had preceded their 71s with a brace of 65s, said that it was "fiendishly difficult" to have great scores back to back.

Els, for his part, read rather more into his third round. His iron play had worried him somewhat, his feeling being that he was aiming a little right of target and hitting over the ball. Against that, he was excited at the way he had married so many smart shots to the slippery links, particularly on and around the greens. "I guess," he said, "that's why we practise our short games so much. You have to be able to hang in there."

The South African was also upbeat about the finish to his round. Like Tiger, he had made birdies at the 16th and 18th. True, the holes were playing short, but the greens, which might have been more difficult to reach in a usual British summer, were shrugging off balls to right and left.

"My finish was a bonus," said Els. "I could easily have shot a 76 or something like that today and yet I am no worse placed than one behind Tiger. I've got to be pleased."

Players Below Par	32
Players At Par	8
Players Above Par	31

American Scott Verplank scored a 67 to jump even higher from the cut line up to a tie for 16th position at six under par. Crane, US Open champion Geoff Ogilvy, Mikko Ilonen, and Tim Clark were among the rest of the pack on the same mark. So was Korea's S K Ho, who played with Lee Westwood, linking their surnames on the scoreboard in a nice homage to Royal North Devon at Westward Ho!, the only golf club in England older than Royal Liverpool.

Greg Owen, who had scored a 67 on Thursday, returned a 68 on Saturday despite re-injuring his back during his warm-up on the practice range. He went to the physiotherapist van for 20 minutes

Unlike some, Phil Mickelson continued to rely heavily on his driver.

of manipulation, took some pain killers, and was able to keep his tee time alongside Phil Mickelson. While the American whaled away with his driver, Owen swung within himself with his irons and six birdies were the result. "It was never a question of whether I would start but whether I could finish," Owen said.

One birdie came from a 60-foot putt at the 11th, and Owen signed off nicely with a birdie from a greenside bunker at the last. It was the only time he was upstaged by Mickelson, whose attempt at charging into contention failed due to the fact that his first birdie came at the 16th. At the last he skipped his hybrid club up to three feet for an eagle, but a 73 had sent him backwards not forwards.

However, Mickelson was ready to offer Owen the advice that he should visit the top back specialist in America and all but produced the phone number as the pair was walking down the second fairway. At the last hole, Owen slipped as he tried to jump out of the bunker and he got back up gingerly, but soon recovered to stand as the leading British player at eight under par. Alongside him were Peter Lonard, Robert Allenby, Jerry Kelly, Retief Goosen, and Andres

Excerpts
FROM THE Press

"Anyone with an ounce of romance about them, who values daring over pragmatism, will be cheering for Angel Cabrera to win The Open at Royal Liverpool."

—**Kevin Mitchell,** *The Observer*

"Though he was born thousands of miles away and lives on the other side of the Atlantic, Tiger Woods is at home here at Royal Liverpool Golf Club."

—**Jim McCabe,** *The Boston Globe*

"Phil Mickelson stumbled to a disappointing 73 to finish a whopping 10 shots behind Tiger Woods—despite a last-hole eagle. The Masters champion struggled hopelessly on Hoylake's greens but promised to shoot low in the final round."

—**Martin Samuel,** *News of the World*

"Golf's greatest closer left the door ajar to The Open. He missed three short putts to invite a bunch of people back into the party."

—**Bill Nichols,** *The Dallas Morning News*

"This has been a week in which Tiger Woods has enrolled in the Jack Nicklaus school of golf to put himself in the driving seat."

—**Neil Silver,** *The People*

"Andrew Marshall took advantage of perfect early morning conditions to post an excellent four-under 68. The 32-year-old from Nottingham was the first man out in the third round."

—**Adam Lanigan,** *The Sunday Post*

Greg Owen played in pain.

A level-par 72 kept Retief Goosen among the top 10.

Romero, an Argentinean who only got into the Championship as the leading non-exempt player in the Scottish Open at Loch Lomond the week before.

Adam Scott, after a 70, and Mark Calcavecchia, the 46-year-old former champion who scored a 68, were at nine under, one behind Tanihara. The 27-year-old from Hiroshima was playing in only his second major championship, having failed to make the cut at Sandwich in The 2003 Open, but holed out from a bunker for a birdie at the 15th and only just missed a long eagle attempt at the last in his 66.

It was the same score achieved by Cabrera, the second Argentinean on the leaderboard hoping to follow in the footsteps of Roberto de Vicenzo from 1967. Cabrera was not born until two years later. "Roberto was a great player and this is a special place, of course," Cabrera said. "But at this moment I am not thinking about history, I'm thinking about Cabrera."

Having gone out in 34, Cabrera enjoyed the best inward half of the day, taking just 32 strokes to get back to the clubhouse. He birdied the 10th and the 12th, three-putted the 13th, but then responded with two more birdies and an eagle at the 16th, where he holed from 15 feet, momentarily to share second place. He finished the day in fifth place with Furyk at 11 under.

For DiMarco, it was another day when he felt the presence of his late mother, Norma. "I know there is divine intervention," he said.

Hideto Tanihara's 66 moved him to seventh.

Peter Lonard tied for 10th on 208.

"I got to the first tee and the name of the scorer was Norma. I've probably met about five Normas in my life. It was weird. As soon as I introduced myself I got goose bumps. I told my caddie, 'She is right there with us.'"

Two late bogeys on the outward nine put him out in 36, one over par, and he had fallen off the pace. But he hit a marvellous wedge shot to four feet at the 11th and that sparked a run of three birdies in a row. He hit a six iron to five feet at the 12th and then a five iron to within three feet at the short 13th. An up-and-down for a birdie 4 at the 16th and he shared the lead with Garcia and Woods. The American aimed to build on his pursuit of Woods at the 2005 Masters and the feeling was that he would not be going away on Sunday.

So even before Woods and Els teed off at 2.30 pm there was reason to believe they could not afford to indulge in a private duel. This was the first time

Andres Romero gave Argentina two Open contenders.

Excerpts FROM THE Press

"Mark Calcavecchia turned back the clock on his glory days as he joined three other Americans near the top of the leaderboard. The 1989 Open winner may be a little more rounded than he was back then. But he still showed he can play great links golf with a sizzling 66."

—**Ken Lawrence**, *Sunday Mirror*

"Why were so many people ready to settle for a protracted coronation when the statistical realities promised a genuine contest of historic possibilities? Yes, obviously, Tiger Woods is why."

—**Hugh McIlvanney**, *The Sunday Times*

"We might have cause to curse him in September but yesterday Chris DiMarco qualified as a local hero as he helped to lead the peloton's attack that cut Tiger Woods's lead to a slender one."

—**Peter Corrigan**,
The Independent on Sunday

"Just when the hopes of a long-awaited European victory in The Open appeared to be fading, Sergio Garcia thrust himself to the fore to remind everyone what an outstanding prospect he used to be."

—**Peter Higgs**, *The Mail on Sunday*

"If Tiger Woods had bothered to look at the flags of 34 countries rippling in the gentle breeze above the grandstands on the 18th hole, he might have noticed that none of them was white."

—**Doug Ferguson**,
The Associated Press

Woods needed a birdie on the 18th to break the first-place tie.

for six years when they had been paired together in the final group at the weekend of a major championship. It never amounted to a classic. Els put his second into a bunker at the first hole to drop a shot, though he got it back at the next. Woods found sand at the second, strangely finding the cross bunker well short of the green to drop a shot and fall back into a share of the lead. He went in front again with a two-putt birdie at the fifth and struck a majestic seven iron to four feet at the short sixth.

The seventh, Telegraph, was a bit of a comedy of errors. Els drove into a bush and had to take an unplayable. His third found a greenside

Round of the **Day**

OFFICIAL SCORECARD
THE OPEN CHAMPIONSHIP 2006
ROYAL LIVERPOOL GOLF CLUB, HOYLAKE

Sergio GARCIA ✓
Game 27
Saturday 22 July at 12:55 pm

FOR R&A USE ONLY   27.2
36 HOLE TOTAL __139__
THIS ROUND __65__
54 HOLE TOTAL 20 4

ROUND 3
54 HOLE TOTAL
204

VERIFIED   C T B

ROUND 3

Hole	1	2	3	4	5	6	7	8	9	Out
Yards	454	436	429	372	528	202	453	423	198	3495
Par	4	4	4	4	5	3	4	4	3	35
Score	4	2	4	4	4	3	3	3	2	29

Hole	10	11	12	13	14	15	16	17	18	In	Total
Yards	534	393	448	198	456	161	554	459	560	3763	7258
Par	5	4	4	3	4	3	5	4	5	37	72
Score	5	4	4	3	4	3	5	4	4	36	65

Signature
of Marker

Signature of
Competitor   Sergio Garcia

Sergio Garcia's round of 65, seven under par, included 29 strokes on the first nine, one off the Championship record for nine holes.

He started with a bang, holing out with his second shot for eagle 2 on the 436-yard second hole. He took a five wood off the tee, then a nine iron from 167 yards for his second. "I just cut it, cut a good solid nine iron there," Garcia said. "As soon as it came out it looked really good. I was hoping for it to be the right distance and I would have a kick-in birdie. It's always nice when you see it go in like that."

Four birdies followed on the outward nine as Garcia became the first player since Ernie Els in 1992 at Muirfield to break 30 for nine holes in The Open.

At the par-5 fifth hole, Garcia hit a driver then a five iron to 20 feet, then two putts. He scored birdies on the last three holes, having wedges to six feet on both the seventh and eighth holes and an eight-iron shot to three feet on the ninth. His only other birdie was on the par-5 closing hole with two putts from 35 feet.

"I was very pleased with the way I played all day, even though on the back nine I only made one birdie," Garcia said. "I felt like I struck the ball very nicely, very solidly all day."

bunker but he got up and down to save bogey. It was the end of a run of 31 holes without dropping a shot. Woods also found a greenside bunker, was right up against the back face and took three to get down, so his lead was cut to one.

Els birdied the ninth but still could not find any rhythm in his game. His short game saved him so that he dropped only one more shot, at the 13th, and he conjured up two more birdies at the two closing par-5s to stay only one behind Woods. "Somehow I hung in there," said the South African. "I could have shot a 76 easily and then I would have been out of it. But I find myself only one behind, so

Geoff Ogilvy, the US Open champion, was seven back.

3

'I was really in control of my game,' said Furyk, who recorded eight birdies in his six-under-par round.

There were 71s, but smiles from Woods and Els in the final pairing.

that's a bonus. I started to get some momentum over the last few holes, so I'll just go with that tomorrow."

Woods began his run for home by three-putting for a par at the 10th, a sign of what was to come. He did, however, hole from 18 feet at the 11th which, after Garcia had posted his 12-under target, got Woods back in front by one. It was a cushion he wasted at the 14th when he charged his first putt four feet past and missed the one back. He got up and down for a 4 at the 16th but then, and this was becoming highly uncharacteristic, he left his birdie effort at the 17th four feet short and missed that, too. He followed that bogey with a two-putt from 40 feet at the last, and a lot of hard work had kept him where he had started the day: one in front.

Each of the three players immediately behind him had duelled with Woods in majors before. Garcia at the 1999 USPGA Championship and the 2002 US Open. Els won the battle for second place when Tiger ran away with the US Open and The Open in 2000. DiMarco pushed Woods to a playoff at the 2005 Masters. But each time Woods had won. "I've done it before," he said. "That's the thing. If you've won before, it always gives you confidence that you can do it again, and I've done it in the past."

Adam Scott was two under par after five holes, and stayed there for a 70.

Tim Clark posted a 69.

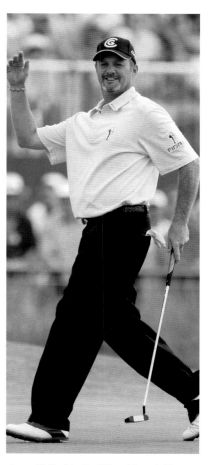

Jerry Kelly birdied Nos 16 and 18.

In the **Words** *of the* **Competitors...**

❝

"Today I hit a lot of good shots, giving myself good chances for birdies, and that's what it's all about."

—Sergio Garcia

"I did a better job adapting to the conditions this year."

—Jim Furyk

"The R&A have done a great job in setting up the course. You've got the world's best golfers rising to the top."

—Adam Scott

"I didn't hit the right shots when I needed to, and I didn't take advantage of the par-5s, and it all added up to 73. But you know, they want it so much, the English players, sometimes it backfires on them."

—Luke Donald

"That's 15 shots to describe, and we might be here for a while (on his two triple bogeys)."

—Paul Casey

"It was a pleasure being there with one of the game's legends (playing with Tom Watson)."

—John Bickerton

❞

Round Three Hole Summary

HOLE	PAR	YARDS	EAGLES	BIRDIES	PARS	BOGEYS	D.BOGEYS	HIGHER	RANK	AVERAGE
1	4	454	0	10	47	13	1	0	9	4.07
2	4	436	2	6	44	17	2	0	5	4.16
3	4	429	0	6	51	12	2	0	7	4.14
4	4	372	0	15	42	13	1	0	11	4.00
5	5	528	4	35	30	2	0	0	17	4.42
6	3	202	0	8	46	15	2	0	5	3.16
7	4	453	0	8	37	23	3	0	4	4.30
8	4	423	0	12	53	6	0	0	13	3.92
9	3	198	0	8	56	7	0	0	12	2.99
OUT	**35**	**3495**	**6**	**108**	**406**	**108**	**11**	**0**		**35.14**
10	5	534	2	42	24	2	0	1	17	4.42
11	4	393	0	17	48	4	0	2	14	3.90
12	4	448	0	4	41	24	1	1	2	4.37
13	3	198	1	7	46	16	0	1	7	3.14
14	4	456	0	5	36	25	3	2	1	4.45
15	3	161	0	7	55	9	0	0	10	3.03
16	5	554	6	35	25	4	0	1	16	4.45
17	4	459	0	3	45	21	2	0	3	4.31
18	5	560	2	32	27	8	2	0	15	4.66
IN	**37**	**3763**	**11**	**152**	**347**	**113**	**8**	**8**		**36.73**
TOTAL	**72**	**7258**	**17**	**260**	**753**	**221**	**19**	**8**		**71.87**

Two over par after three holes, Robert Allenby returned a 69 with five birdies.

A Brave Face On A Brave Experiment

High on the list of sentences that Phil Mickelson would never want to utter would be the following, spoken quite early on Saturday afternoon after his 73 in the third round. "This," he said, "is going to be an interesting day to watch the leaders play."

Whoa there. Who is this saying: "To watch the leaders play?" Surely not the Phil Mickelson who flew thousands of miles, spent thousands of pounds and hundreds of hours preparing as no man had ever done before for The Open, in the high expectation that the only leaders he would be watching would be those alongside him in contention for the Claret Jug?

Well, yes, it was the very same Mickelson, who was in the process of proving that no amount of preparation can help unless you play the shots and hole the putts. The American, having started reasonably enough with rounds of 69 and 71, had just taken a one-over-par 73 and had decelerated sharply down the leaderboard. Now came the realisation that he had no chance of winning, a fact that was made harder to take by the further fact that the actual leaders had only just gone out and he would indeed be able to spend the rest of the afternoon watching them.

Mickelson, uniquely, had made a special flight from America to Hoylake three weeks before the Championship to examine minutely a links that none of the players knew. Then, rather than play in the Barclays Scottish Open at Loch Lomond, he arrived in Liverpool early, and by the time he teed off for the first round had played the course 10 times.

It was a nice try, but there was to be no cigar. Dave Pelz, his short game guru, said after the third round, "He's struggling. The iron shots that are supposed to end up close aren't happening. It doesn't matter

how good the game plan is if you don't execute. I know I would be very frustrated, but Phil is taking it very well."

Indeed, he was putting a brave face on the failure of an experiment that was itself brave; an attempt to understand the mysteries of Hoylake to a greater extent than anyone else, which had been derailed by the very nature of golf, where to play

well deliberately is simply not possible.

That third round, for instance, had been close to being really bad. He was four over par after 14 holes, by which time he was telling himself, "I realised the chances of winning were no longer there, so I just tried to hit good shots and see if I could turn things around."

At least he managed that. A birdie at the long 16th was followed by an eagle at the long 18th, where, from 245 yards out he hit a hybrid club, "a three iron or four wood," and finished just three feet away. It

was a lifting note on which to finish, albeit garnished with a little luck—the second shot ran perilously close to a greenside bunker before taking the contours to end up close.

Mickelson, though, was endeavouring to be philosophical. Asked if it was frustrating to be getting such a poor result from so much effort, he said, "It's really not that bad. I enjoy my job. I enjoy practising and working on the golf course and competing in the event, so it's fun for me."

But for a competitor with a will to win as strong as Mickelson's, being tied for 39th place after three rounds was not where he wanted to be, could not have been fun. "There are a lot of birdies out there," he admitted, "because the wind has not been as strong as we were expecting. But even so it is hard to get the ball to three, four or five feet from the hole, which means that you're facing 15- or 20-footers, and I just didn't hole any of those.

"There are birdie holes out there, the fourth and all the par-5s are reachable. You know, I don't feel as if I've been making bogeys and falling behind, just that I haven't made the birdies."

So what, now that the immaculate preparation had failed? Mickelson said that he was already looking ahead. "I want to play a good round here and move on. But before I do that I want to get together one good round of golf—not just to move me up the leaderboard, but more for self-gratification. I just want to play this course well for one round."

Footnote: A final round of 70 was not what Mickelson was looking for. "I struck the ball okay," he said despondently, "but the putting…"

—**David Davies**

Fourth Round

This One's For Dad

By Andy Farrell

The year The Open came back to Hoylake belonged to Tiger Woods with a splendid defence of his title for his third Open victory and his 11th major championship as a professional.

A gorgeous sunset sealed this memorable week on the Wirral, viewed by most in their rear view mirrors as they drove away from the course. Not Tiger Woods, however. He set sail into it later in the evening on his private jet. He was always in the right place at the right time during The 135th Open Championship. Accompanying Tiger was a most prized piece of luggage. The Claret Jug arrived with Woods and departed safely in his hands after the most majestic exhibition of ball-striking over the Hoylake links.

As calm and clinical and controlled a performance as it was, this was also Tiger's most emotional victory, the first since the death of his father, Earl, in May.

In an emotional finish, Tiger Woods won his third Open.

The standing ovation afforded the champion at the 72nd hole of any Open is always an awe-inspiring occasion, and amid the rapture Steve Williams, his caddie, turned to Woods as they approached the green and said, "This one's for dad."

Tiger, not ready to crack, kept himself in check until he had tapped in to confirm a two-stroke winning margin. He observed the etiquette of shaking the hands of his playing companion, Sergio Garcia, and Garcia's caddie. But then Woods wrapped Williams in a huge bear hug. The tears came then and the embrace continued. Finally, he tore himself away, but only to find the arms of his wife, Elin, and his coach, Hank Haney.

For all the statistical and historical meaning that would be attached to this victory, for Woods there was only one overwhelming feeling. "After the last putt, I realised that my dad is never going to see this again," Woods said at the presentation ceremony.

"I wish he could have seen this one last time. I tried hard at Augusta but it didn't quite happen. He was out there today keeping me calm. I had a calm feeling the entire week, especially today. I love my dad and I miss him so much. To win my first

4

Fourth Round Leaders

HOLE	1	2	3	4	5	6	7	8	9	10	11	12	13	14	15	16	17	18	TOTAL
PAR	4	4	4	4	5	3	4	4	3	5	4	4	3	4	3	5	4	5	TOTAL
Tiger Woods	4	4	4	4	(3)	3	4	4	3	(4)	4	[5]	3	(3)	(2)	(4)	4	5	67-270
Chris DiMarco	[5]	4	4	4	5	(2)	4	4	3	(4)	4	4	(2)	4	3	(4)	4	(4)	68-272
Ernie Els	4	4	4	4	(4)	3	4	[5]	3	5	[5]	4	3	(3)	3	(4)	4	5	71-275
Jim Furyk	[5]	[5]	4	4	5	3	[5]	4	3	(4)	4	4	3	4	(2)	(4)	4	(4)	71-276
Hideto Tanihara	4	(3)	4	4	[6]	[5]	4	4	(2)	5	4	(3)	3	(3)	3	(4)	[5]	5	71-277
Sergio Garcia	4	[5]	[5]	4	5	3	4	[5]	[4]	5	4	(3)	3	[5]	(2)	(3)	4	5	73-277
Angel Cabrera	4	[7]	4	4	(4)	3	4	4	3	(4)	4	[5]	[4]	4	3	(4)	4	(4)	73-278
Carl Pettersson	[5]	4	[6]	4	(4)	3	(3)	4	3	(3)	4	4	3	[5]	(2)	(4)	4	(4)	69-279
Andres Romero	4	4	4	(3)	(4)	(2)	4	4	[4]	5	(3)	4	[4]	[5]	3	(4)	[5]	5	71-279
Adam Scott	[5]	[5]	(3)	4	(4)	3	4	4	(2)	(4)	[5]	4	3	4	(2)	(4)	[5]	[7]	72-279
Anthony Wall	4	4	(3)	4	5	3	(3)	4	3	(4)	4	4	3	4	3	5	[5]	(4)	69-280
Ben Crane	4	4	4	(3)	5	[4]	4	4	3	5	4	4	3	4	(2)	(4)	4	5	70-280
S K Ho	4	4	4	4	(4)	3	4	4	(2)	(4)	[5]	4	[4]	4	3	(4)	[5]	(4)	70-280
Sean O'Hair	4	4	4	4	(4)	3	4	4	(2)	(4)	4	4	3	[5]	3	(4)	(3)	(4)	67-281
Retief Goosen	4	[5]	4	4	5	[4]	4	4	3	(4)	4	[5]	3	[5]	(2)	(4)	4	5	73-281

Ernie Els said he 'let it slip' on the eighth to 11th holes.

tournament after my dad passed away, and for it to be a major championship, it makes it that much more special."

Perhaps there had not been quite the drama that had been anticipated with a round to play. The record will state that for the 11th time Woods took a lead, or a share of the lead, into the last round of a major championship and for the 11th time he won. He led by one and then matched the best score of the final round with a 67. Periods of awed quiet hung over the links, punctuated by mighty roars, but both extremes of auditory sensation honoured a special performance from the defending champion. It was one that combined the meticulous resolve of the 18 pars produced by Nick Faldo at Muirfield in 1987 and the ruthless surge to quell any counterattack.

At one point on the inward nine Chris DiMarco got within a stroke, but Woods responded by making three birdies in a row. "Hey, Tiger, would you just give me a little chance for once," DiMarco said to Woods outside the recorder's hut. They both shared a laugh.

Sunday Weather
Sunny periods with a northwesterly breeze in the afternoon.

Over the closing holes, Chris DiMarco was left as the final challenger and was three strokes ahead of third place.

"He's got an uncanny ability, when someone gets close to him, to turn it up another level," DiMarco added later. The American had chased Tiger home at the Masters in 2005 before losing in a playoff. This was the third occasion when he had finished runner-up in a major championship.

Woods, however, had added to his list of triumphs. This was his third victory in The Open Championship following wins at St Andrews in 2000 and 2005. He became the 19th player to hold the Claret Jug three times, joining Jack Nicklaus and Faldo, among others. He was the first player since Tom Watson at Royal Birkdale in 1983 to win in defence of the title. Nodding at the Jug, Tiger said, "It's a pretty sweet feeling to have this for an entire year at home."

In all it was his 11th professional major championship, bringing him alongside Walter Hagen in the all-time list and moving him one nearer to his target of Nicklaus's 18 titles. Hagen also won The Open at Hoylake, in 1924. The 11th and last major title of his career—Hagen did not have the Masters to play in at that time—came in 1929 at Muirfield. It was his fourth Open triumph and, like Tiger here, he was winning back-to-back titles after victory at Sandwich the previous year.

It's a
Fact

Tiger Woods has now tied Walter Hagen with 11 professional major championships, and they are second on the list behind Jack Nicklaus and his 18 major victories. Following them are Ben Hogan and Gary Player, each with nine professional majors, and Tom Watson with eight.

Excerpts
FROM THE Press

"Tiger Woods had an answer for everyone in another methodical march to victory in The Open. One month after missing the cut for the first time in a major, Woods was as ruthless as ever on the brown-baked links of Royal Liverpool, making three straight birdies to turn away a spirited challenge by Chris DiMarco and win golf's oldest championship for the second straight year."

—Doug Ferguson, *The Associated Press*

"Sam Torrance and Mark James, two European Ryder Cup captains, were among the luminaries at Hoylake who hailed the golf played by Tiger Woods en route to his third Open Championship as the finest they had seen from him."

—Ian Chadband, *Evening Standard*

"Given that he was the only European to get close to contending, Sergio Garcia's eventual tied-fifth finish at least improved his status on the European Ryder Cup points list."

—Philip Reid, *The Irish Times*

"Anthony Wall, the son of a London cabbie, and a diehard Queen's Park Rangers fan, rounded off a superb personal performance by compiling a 69 to finish eight under par in a tie for 11th place."

—Nick Harris, *The Independent*

"In the end only Chris DiMarco among a chasing pack including the likes of Sergio Garcia, Ernie Els, and Jim Furyk offered anything approaching a worthwhile challenge."

—Lawrence Donegan, *The Guardian*

Jim Furyk started with two bogeys.

Marius Thorp led the amateurs.

Nicklaus's 11th professional major came at the 1972 US Open. He had already won the Masters that year and lost narrowly to Lee Trevino at Muirfield in The Open. His 12th title had to wait until the USPGA Championship the following year. There was little to suggest here that Tiger would not be adding a 12th triumph, and sooner rather than later.

The 12th for Nicklaus was also his 14th overall, including two US Amateur titles, to pass Bobby Jones and his total of 13, then the record. That achievement was widely applauded in 1973, but in the years since, professional majors have become the standard. Woods now has 14 overall, including his three US Amateur victories.

At the age of 30, Woods already has a career which has inspired many youngsters. One of them was waiting at the presentation ceremony. Marius Thorp, the 18-year-old reigning European Amateur champion from Norway, took up the game after watching Tiger on television. The son of a famous Norwegian football referee, Thorp won the Silver Medal as the lowest amateur—US Amateur champion Edoardo Molinari was his only contender over the weekend—and enjoyed a final round with five-time Open champion Tom Watson.

Challenges That Failed To Materialise

'Nothing seemed to go my way,' Garcia says

When Sergio Garcia left his first putt on the first green of the final round some six feet short, there was a bit of a gasp from the gallery. Then the Spaniard holed it for a par and there were murmurs of approval. Perhaps most people in that gallery wanted Tiger Woods to be tested and, as the man with whom he was paired, Garcia was best placed to exert some pressure.

So, as the players left for the second tee, the question hung in the air: Which was the real Garcia, the one who had hit a pitiful first putt or the one who had impressively holed the second?

Unfortunately, for all those who wanted some drama in the day's proceedings, it was to be the former. Although Garcia's six-footer had gone into the middle of the hole at exactly the right pace, it failed to give him the confidence he needed to take on the world's best golfer. He immediately three-putted the next two greens, and if Garcia occasionally brings the bravery and the brilliance of the matador to his golf game, this time he was gored by his own sword.

"I thought I had hit good putts," Garcia said, "but they didn't go in. Nothing seemed to go my way."

For those with an acquaintance with the statistics it was not a surprise. Garcia, even as an amateur, was not a great putter, and although he has occasional passages of success, overall he has not improved in his seven years as a professional. For

Sergio Garcia could not overcome a poor start.

Ernie Els posted three birdies but fell short.

instance, out of the 194 members of the USPGA Tour recorded in the putting statistics, Garcia was 179th before The Open, a figure that simply cannot be equated with success.

Neither can his final-round stroke average. For the first three rounds of a tournament Garcia averages 71.8, 71.2, and 71.5 strokes. For the fourth round it is 73.89 strokes, another unsustainable statistic.

So any suggestion of a challenge from Garcia failed to materialise, as, in the end, did anything from Ernie Els. The South African sustained a nasty injury to his left knee almost exactly a year before The Open, and while he appears to be able to walk comfortably enough, there is the occasional suggestion of favouring that leg at the completion of the swing.

Although Els birdied the long fifth to move to 13 under par and be tied with Woods, who was playing behind him, the response from the South African when Tiger eagled that same hole, was to drop two shots. He was never a factor in the Championship after that, his 71 leaving him five behind Woods, and while he was third overall, meaning five top-three finishes in seven years, it was not the win that Els and his talent crave.

"I haven't had a great time on the golf course the last year or so, but I've done a lot of work," Els said. "I'm starting to feel the vibes again, so to speak, and I'm looking forward to the future."

—David Davies

"

"Today I played with one of the biggest legends in the game in Tom Watson, and that was simply fantastic. I learned so much today, and it's been a perfect day so far."

—Marius Thorp (winner of the Silver Medal)

"To finish like that (69) was brilliant for me. It's been great here."

—Anthony Wall

"Obviously, I'm pretty disappointed. My putter just completely did me in this weekend."

—Graeme McDowell

"This is by far my biggest achievement. I never expected to be in the top 10, but I did expect to play well this week."

—Hideto Tanihara

"I struggled to get the ball in the hole, and in the majors you have to putt well."

—Phil Mickelson

"It's been a reasonable week for me. I wish I had brought more game here."

—Geoff Ogilvy

Hideto Tanihara had the second-best finish ever by a Japanese player.

Both closed with rounds of 71 to finish on level par.

Long before Thorp got his wish to meet Tiger at the presentation ceremony, there was much else to be decided. Paul Broadhurst, out in 32, hinted at a charge, but his two eagles were cancelled out by two double bogeys. He finished at four under par. Greg Owen closed with a 75 to fall back to five under, one behind Robert Rock. Sean O'Hair, from America, birdied the last three holes for a 67 which stood as the best score of the day until Woods matched it. He finished at seven under, alongside Retief Goosen.

Anthony Wall ended the Championship as the leading British player at eight under par, alongside Ben Crane and S K Ho. He closed with a 69, but had his eagle attempt at the last dropped, as it promised to do, he would have crept into the top 10. Instead, he will have to find another way of qualifying for next year's Open at Carnoustie. That will not be a problem for Andres Romero, the Argentinean playing in his first Open, and Hideto Tanihara, of Japan.

Tanihara closed with a 71 and finished in fifth place alongside Garcia and one outside the best-ever result by a Japanese player in The Open Championship; Masahiro Kuramoto tied for fourth in 1982. Romero, who had only qualified at the Barclays Scottish Open the week before, tied for eighth with Carl Pettersson and Adam Scott, who dropped three strokes in the last two holes.

It was fitting for Argentina to have two representatives in the top 10 at the venue of Roberto de Vicenzo's win in 1967. Angel Cabrera's

Carl Pettersson recorded three birdies in the last four holes.

Following John Bickerton here, Dave Musgrove was the only returning caddie from The Open in 1967.

Anthony Wall was the low British player on 280.

hopes of matching his illustrious countryman ended when he took a triple-bogey 7 at the second hole. He took two to escape from a fairway bunker and was still in the rough at that stage. Cabrera's playing companion, Jim Furyk, also had a poor start, bogeying the first two holes, and only three birdies in the last four holes hauled the American up to 12 under and fourth place, matching his results in 1997 and 1998.

So the contest was down to the final two groups on the course, DiMarco and Ernie Els, and Woods and Garcia. The world No 1, one ahead of the other three, sported his usual red-tinted Sunday shirt. Garcia was dressed head to foot in canary yellow. DiMarco dropped a shot at the first, but it was to be his only bogey of the day. Garcia missed a short putt at the second, his first bogey for 24 holes, but unlike the American he could not limit the damage.

Andres Romero (above) and Angel Cabrera gave Argentina two players in the top 10, appropriately for Hoylake.

Ben Crane posted a 70 to finish eight under par.

Sean O'Hair scored birdies on the last three holes for a 67.

Another even shorter putt slipped by at the third and suddenly all the confidence in the 26-year-old Spaniard's game seemed to evaporate. It was not the first time that his stunning iron play has been let down by his putting, especially in the final round of a tournament. He stuck with the left-hand-below-right method, but between putts appeared to be thinking about trying different styles. "Those two three-putts put me a bit on the defensive," Garcia said. "I thought I hit good putts but they didn't go in."

Although Garcia had challenged Woods at the 1999 USPGA Championship, the only time he had played with Tiger in the final group of a major championship was at the 2002 US Open. "I can take a lot of positives out of this tournament," he said. "It's probably the best I've felt in a major

His Mother 'Would Be Proud'

Chris DiMarco started his fourth round one shot behind Tiger Woods, in the pairing with Ernie Els in front of the world No 1. While Woods was determined to win for his late father, DiMarco was no less intent on honouring his mother, who had died two weeks prior to the Championship.

Woods was coldly determined, while DiMarco, though he had talked of "this great sense of peace" which surrounded him, was pumped up.

The crux of the afternoon came when DiMarco holed for his birdie from 20 feet at the 13th to go to 14 under par. Woods, who was playing the 12th at the time, mis-cued with his second shot and opted for a sensible chip, one which would pave the way for a possible par and a certain bogey, rather than leave him impossibly placed through the green. He made the bogey and, at that point, his lead was cut to one.

DiMarco drove into the worst of the rough at the 14th, and it looked as if he had taken fright at such a turn of events. Not a bit of it… After catching the green with his second shot, he holed the putt, trium-phantly, from 15 yards to stay on Woods's heels.

Yet, though Woods would talk after-wards about how conscious he was of DiMarco pushing him all the way, he was above being influenced by anyone or anything. He hit a breathtaking five iron to nine feet at the 14th on his way to the

birdie with which he retrieved his two-shot lead.

Another thrust from DiMarco was needed and, sure enough, he holed from 15 feet for a birdie at the 16th, to cut the margin to one again. So hyped up was DiMarco at this point that he inadvertently stole Els's honour on the 17th tee. Els let it go, though he did protest, albeit gently, when the American was poised to do the same again at the 18th.

By now, the buzz surrounding DiMarco would almost certainly have had its effect on anyone other than Woods. As it was, Tiger's cocoon of concentration was no closer to being pierced. Having birdied the 14th, he added two more at the 15th and 16th, thereby having the breathing space he wanted for the last two holes.

Afterwards, DiMarco would talk about Woods's "uncanny ability to turn his game up to another level" whenever that was required.

He heaped praise on Woods but could not be anything but positive about his own day's work. He had come storming up the Ryder Cup points list, and he had given the kind of performance of which he said his mother "would be very proud of me right now. One, for playing well, but two, just

because that's the way she was."

"I played great," DiMarco said, while noting that he had been five under par for his last 13 holes. Being up against Woods, it was suggested, seemed to spell the end for the rest where it had brought the best out of him. "If you can't get up playing the best player in the world in a major, you never will," he said.

As Tiger once said, DiMarco continued, "being in contention in a major, or any tournament, is like a drug, and it is. It is our drug."

—Lewine Mair

---

with the putter stroke." But for the first three days he had made his score, 12 under, on the outward nine, while he had played the inward nine in level par. Now he would go out in 39, 10 more strokes than the previous day.

Woods, after his putting hiccups on Saturday, was rolling his ball beautifully and on the opening holes saw a number of chances only just miss. He parred the first four holes, as did Els ahead of him. The South African two-putted from off the front edge of the fifth green for a birdie 4 and was tied with

Woods at 13 under. Tiger responded immediately, as is his wont. He bashed a pair of two-iron shots onto the green at the fifth and holed from 12 feet for an eagle. Suddenly, he was two clear again.

DiMarco retrieved his dropped shot from the first with a beautiful tee shot at the short sixth, but an outward half of 35, level par, left him three behind. That became the margin of Tiger's lead when Els bogeyed the eighth. He miscued his approach to the eighth and looked to the heavens with scrunched up eyes. His recovery came out to 10 feet but he

4

After four bogeys in the first nine holes, Sergio Garcia had fallen six strokes off the lead.

Players Below Par	27
Players At Par	9
Players Above Par	35

Low Scores

Low First Nine
Paul Broadhurst	32

Low Second Nine
John Senden	33
Jim Furyk	33
Carl Pettersson	33
Chris DiMarco	33

Low Round
Sean O'Hair	67
Tiger Woods	67

missed the par effort. He, too, was out in 35, and Woods was able to collect pars at the next few holes to complete a first nine of 33 strokes, while Garcia suffered two more bogeys at the eighth and ninth.

Garcia was finally able to spread his arms in celebration of a birdie at the 12th, but not before going seven behind. He bogeyed the 14th before a birdie at the 15th and an eagle at the 16th. A 73 left him back at 11 under with Tanihara.

At the par-5 10th, Far, Els found the front-right bunker but played a fine recovery to four feet. Alas, he missed the putt and had to settle for a par. At the next, he sought the pin at the back of the green but went over and took three to get down. It was a crucial bogey. He was now five behind. "That four-hole stretch, eight to 11, that's where it got away," Els admitted. "It is not a very tough stretch, but I made two bogeys instead of two birdies. If I had played them in two under par instead of two over, I'd have had half a chance. But Tiger played great today."

Els picked up a birdie at the fearsome 14th with a superb approach to four feet and then took a 4 at the 16th, but a 71 left the 2002

When it seemed DiMarco might drop a shot at the 14th, he holed from 40 feet.

In the *Words* of the *Competitors...*

"We've talked about my form at The Open being dismal over the last few years, so to come out and play well this week and get in the top five, it was a good, solid week."

—Jim Furyk

"I was getting bigger cheers than Tiger on some of the holes and that was a great thing for me to experience. That's why this is my favourite event. It's just different."

—Sergio Garcia

"It is awesome to be playing well and performing well when everything is on the line."

—Chris DiMarco

"Every time I was in the bunkers I started calling them roundabouts because of the direction you were hitting the ball."

—David Duval

"I didn't have control of the golf ball this week. And if you don't have control of the golf ball around here, you're not going to get away with it."

—Paul Casey

champion in third place at 13 under. If there was a consolation it was in finding himself back in contention at a major for the first time since that nasty knee injury in the summer of 2005. "It's been a struggle for almost a year, so to play some decent golf again was a thrill," he said.

Tiger's only challenger left was DiMarco, one of the few men to have outscored Woods in the final round of a major while playing alongside him. That was at the 2005 Masters, but this time he was in the group ahead. At the 10th he put a three iron onto the green

Expecting this 18-foot putt to fall for eagle on the 16th, Woods scored his third consecutive birdie and led by three.

and two-putted for a birdie to get within two, but Woods had him covered. At the same hole Tiger had only a six iron for his approach shot, downwind, and though he leaned as if the ball might fall off the green, it stayed on. He two-putted from 35 feet to reach 16 under and go three ahead again.

DiMarco made an important par save at the 11th and then holed from 20 feet for a birdie at the short 13th. This time Woods could not maintain his advantage. About to play his approach at the 12th, Woods had to back off the shot due to some errant camera clicks. "Come on, have some consideration for the players, please," barked Williams. It was not just here. The whole round spectators had been clicking away with cameras and camera-phones, a distraction which led to the final pairing being put on the clock, a warning of slow play, between the 10th and 12th holes.

It was all part of the enthusiasm the local area had shown for

Championship Totals	
Players Below Par	190
Players At Par	53
Players Above Par	210

Round Four Hole Summary

HOLE	PAR	YARDS	EAGLES	BIRDIES	PARS	BOGEYS	D.BOGEYS	HIGHER	RANK	AVERAGE
1	4	454	0	4	48	16	3	0	4	4.25
2	4	436	0	2	41	26	1	1	1	4.41
3	4	429	0	4	55	10	2	0	11	4.14
4	4	372	0	5	61	5	0	0	12	4.00
5	5	528	3	26	30	12	0	0	15	4.72
6	3	202	0	6	39	19	7	0	2	3.38
7	4	453	0	7	44	18	2	0	7	4.21
8	4	423	0	6	52	10	2	1	8	4.17
9	3	198	0	13	49	8	1	0	13	2.96
OUT	**35**	**3495**	**3**	**73**	**419**	**124**	**18**	**2**		**36.24**
10	5	534	4	32	32	3	0	0	17	4.48
11	4	393	0	7	49	11	4	0	8	4.17
12	4	448	0	6	45	17	2	1	4	4.25
13	3	198	0	5	51	14	1	0	10	3.16
14	4	456	0	12	34	20	5	0	4	4.25
15	3	161	0	20	41	10	0	0	14	2.86
16	5	554	3	41	20	6	1	0	18	4.45
17	4	459	0	2	44	22	3	0	3	4.37
18	5	560	1	29	33	5	3	0	15	4.72
IN	**37**	**3763**	**8**	**154**	**349**	**108**	**19**	**1**		**36.71**
TOTAL	**72**	**7258**	**11**	**227**	**768**	**232**	**37**	**3**		**72.94**

the return of The Open to Hoylake. Over 230,000 spectators attended over the week, a record for an Open in England. "It's the people who have made this week, and it's felt very much like a people's Open," said Thomas Bjorn. Just a few too many, however, wanted their own private memento of the occasion.

Woods regrouped, as he is always able to do, but his four-iron approach slipped down the bank to the right of the 12th green. "I didn't mis-hit any shots today," Woods said. "I may have started the ball left or right a couple of times, but they were hit flush, which is a pretty neat feeling." He was the last player standing who had not dropped a shot in the final round, but his chip ran 15 feet past the hole and his only bogey of the day followed.

Now DiMarco was only one shot back, but he looked to be in trouble when his three-iron approach at the 14th stayed up in the rough on a bank short-left of the green. It was a horrid lie and he could only chop the ball onto the putting surface. Then something amazing happened. He rolled in the putt from well over 40 feet and saved par. "It was a great putt and really pumped me up," the American said.

Woods, however, came up with something even more amazing. At the same 14th hole where he had holed out for an eagle on Friday, he now hit a sublime approach with a five iron to nine feet, pin-high left of the hole and made a 3. His tee shot with a nine iron at the next, the short 15th, got a helpful nudge off the ridge on the left of the green and finished 10 feet away for a birdie 2. Tiger then powered his ball onto the green at the par-5 16th,

4

Excerpts
FROM THE Press

"Sergio Garcia walked to the first tee of The Open and heard cheering worthy of a World Cup goal. He split the first fairway, outdriving Tiger Woods by 30 yards, using a driver to Woods's three wood. He matched Woods with an opening par. And then Garcia's game went south."

—**Damon Hack,** *The New York Times*

"Alas, for his many friends and admirers, come the climax of The Open, Ernie Els was the nearly man yet again, finishing in the top three for the fifth time in seven years after a humdrum (for him) last round of 71."

—**Robert Philip,** *The Daily Telegraph*

"Chris DiMarco accepted the compensation of a return ticket to the Ryder Cup after again being denied his first major by the brilliance of Tiger Woods."

—**Neil McLeman,** *Daily Mirror*

"When the four-day, 72-hole clinic had been completed, and the tears had stopped flowing and the emotions were finally in check, Tiger Woods was asked to sum up his feelings after his third Open victory had been completed in grand style. He took a deep breath and said, 'I don't know where to begin.'"

—**Jim McCabe,** *The Boston Globe*

"Tiger Woods spent The Open redefining the human limits of control on a golf course."

—**Steve Campbell,** *Houston Chronicle*

Caddie Steve Williams was there to comfort Woods at the finish.

pin-high left, with a three wood off the tee and a seven iron on the approach, then his trademark twirl of the club when he knows a good one is on the way, and the eagle putt from 18 feet only just missed.

Those three birdies in a row had once again staked an indisputable claim to the title. DiMarco, arriving at the 16th first, had got his 4 there despite coming up short in the rough with his second, and he chipped and putted for another 4 at the last. A closing 68 was a brave effort, but 16 under was not enough.

DiMarco was watched by his father, Rich, and son, Cristian, and the threesome were all grieving for a lost wife, mother, and grandma. "Chris played a magnificent round of golf and kept the pressure on me," Woods said to the 18th gallery. "Everyone sends best wishes to you and your entire family for what you are going through right now."

Woods parred the last two holes, just missing from six feet on the 18th after a two iron off the tee and a four iron for his second shot. Had he made that birdie he would have tied his own record for The Open of 19 under par. While there was plenty of low scoring over the links of Royal Liverpool, not a single new scoring record for the Championship was set during the week. It was a triumphant return to Hoylake for the first time since 1967. "This has been a fantastic week for all the players to be able to play this course," Woods said.

"It has been a fantastic Championship and the course was a fantastic test of golf. With the course being this fast, it lent itself to amazing creativity." Woods said his late father would have loved seeing him develop a game plan for the particular examination presented and then stick to it, grinding his

Round of the Day

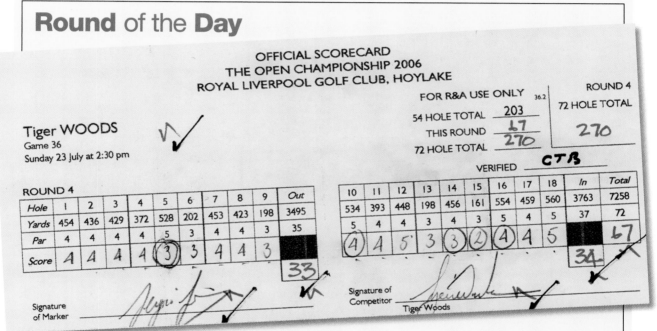

Never wavering from his conservative plan, Tiger Woods didn't take the headcover off his driver in the final round—and he did so only once all week, on the 16th hole on the first day—while recording a 67 to win his third Open title by two strokes. He finished the week with the most fairways hit (48 of a possible 54) and tied for the second most greens in regulation (58 of a possible 72).

"The golf course allowed you to run the ball up on basically every hole," Woods said. "You had an opportunity to run the ball on the green, so I just took advantage of that."

Starting with four pars, Woods hit a two iron off the tee on the par-5 fifth then another two iron into the green, and scored an eagle 3 on a 15-foot putt, and was out in 33. At the par-5 10th, Woods took a three wood off the tee, a six iron to the green, and two putts from 35 feet for a birdie. He made a bogey on the 12th when his approach shot slipped off the green, his chip ran 15 feet past the hole, and he missed the putt.

Chris DiMarco was within one stroke, but then came three birdies in succession by Woods—a five iron to nine feet on the 14th, a nine iron to 10 feet on the 15th, and a seven iron to 18 feet and two putts on the par-5 16th. That was all he needed.

Championship Hole Summary

HOLE	PAR	YARDS	EAGLES	BIRDIES	PARS	BOGEYS	D.BOGEYS	HIGHER	RANK	AVERAGE
1	4	454	0	45	291	102	15	1	7	4.20
2	4	436	2	37	261	140	11	3	3	4.29
3	4	429	0	42	307	88	11	6	8	4.19
4	4	372	0	57	331	61	5	0	11	4.03
5	5	528	23	205	185	36	5	0	16	4.55
6	3	202	0	33	314	90	17	0	6	3.20
7	4	453	0	52	270	112	17	3	5	4.23
8	4	423	0	58	336	52	5	2	13	4.02
9	3	198	0	63	321	62	6	1	11	3.03
OUT	**35**	**3495**	**25**	**592**	**2616**	**743**	**92**	**16**		**35.74**
10	5	534	16	239	171	19	7	1	17	4.48
11	4	393	0	71	306	68	6	2	10	4.03
12	4	448	0	21	275	138	15	4	1	4.35
13	3	198	1	46	308	91	5	2	9	3.13
14	4	456	1	35	261	129	22	5	2	4.33
15	3	161	1	77	321	51	3	0	14	2.95
16	5	554	27	252	139	33	1	1	18	4.41
17	4	459	0	26	292	122	11	1	4	4.27
18	5	560	10	200	194	35	10	4	15	4.66
IN	**37**	**3763**	**56**	**967**	**2267**	**686**	**81**	**20**		**36.63**
TOTAL	**72**	**7258**	**81**	**1559**	**4883**	**1429**	**173**	**36**		**72.37**

way along his chosen path. In a week where the wind turbines out in the Dee estuary appeared to be on a go slow, the course's defences were the bunkering and the difficulty of the hole locations. Woods decided to go without his driver, using the club only once during the week. In doing so he not only came second in terms of greens in regulation, something that is no surprise, but had the best percentage of fairways hit, something he has not managed for years.

It did not matter that Woods was 53rd in distance off the tees, averaging 290.9 yards to leader Andrew Buckle's 320.8.

If Woods did not need his driver, then at least it made a change from all the driver-wedge golf that is seen in modern golf. To force the world No 1 to adapt his usual game plan, and then see him execute it perfectly with a flawless performance of long and mid-iron striking, is credit enough. It was Bernard Darwin who wrote in praise of Hoylake that it was "blown upon by mighty winds" and was a "breeder of mighty champions." The former might not have applied in 2006, but the latter sentiment certainly did.

The Claret Jug, as usual engraved by the time the champion received it—for the first time by Garry Harvey, the 1972 British Boys champion, having taken over from his father, Alex, who held the job from 1960—was back in Tiger's possession. "The Jug will be filled up," Woods said of the celebrations to come, "with a beverage of my choice. And not just once."

"Tiger Woods's golf seems to intimidate other players, an intangible influence that seems to stifle them, even when they are playing a different part of the course. But Chris DiMarco? He seems steeled to its effect, belligerently refusing to bow to its force."

—**Owen Slot**, *The Times*

"Tiger Woods controlled his golf ball as well as, if not better than, he ever has, but as soon as he holed the clinching putt in The Open, he couldn't control his emotions."

—**Dave Anderson**, *The New York Times*

"Didn't you love it, Earl? Wasn't it something the way your kid again lived up to your promises and our expectations? You watched it from up there, the way you used to watch down here, didn't you?"

—**Art Spander**, *Oakland Tribune*

"The muscle man was replaced by the thinker as Tiger Woods produced a masterclass to romp to his 11th major title."

—**David Facey**, *The Sun*

"After two days in the sun with Tiger Woods earlier this week, Nick Faldo was back in his American television commentary booth while Woods was busy trying to secure yet another title."

—**Matthew Dunn**, *Daily Express*

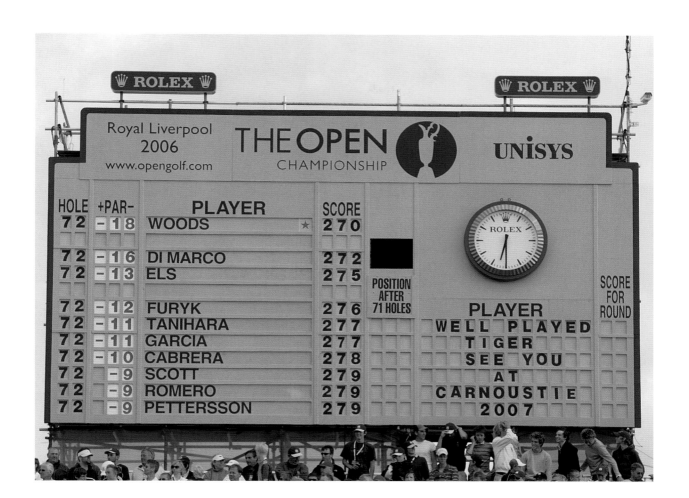

Abiding Memories Of Hoylake

By John Hopkins

There was something appropriate about Tiger Woods winning The Open in this year and at this place, an historic winner at an historic venue. His victory gave a sense of normality being restored to the game. Who better to anoint Hoylake on its return to The Open rota after a 39-year absence than a Woods who was in the imperious form he had last demonstrated in the early years of the century? How better for Woods to show that he had come to terms with the death two months earlier of his father, his mentor, and best friend, than by winning by two strokes and then breaking down in tears and dedicating the victory to him.

The bare bones of Woods's victory are that his rounds of 67, 65, 71, and 67 totalled 270, 18 under par, one less than the record for a major championship that Woods himself set in the 2000 Open at St Andrews. He equalled the course record of 65 set by Chris DiMarco and also equalled by Ernie Els and Sergio Garcia and took his total of major championships to 11, equalling Walter Hagen. Jack Nicklaus's total of 18 professional major championships is the only record still in Woods's sights.

Rarely have bare bones hidden so many secrets, however. If Woods's dominance over the assembled cast was wondrous for spectators to behold, and it was, it must have been frightening for his peers. Rarely has a sportsman demonstrated his superiority over his rivals with such controlled power. Even a comparatively poor demonstration on the greens on Saturday, when he three-putted three times in his last eight holes, did not take the shine off his victory.

As early as the first practice round Woods and Hank Haney, his coach, worked out that a typical Woods drive on the brown, firm fairways would send the ball 370 or 380 yards, but unless it was accurate it would roll into the rough. Better to

play short of the menacing, penal fairway bunkers and make sure of playing from the fairway, the two men thought. From that moment on, Woods plotted his way round as a navigator does the passage of a ship. He used two or three irons from the tees of the par-4s and his three wood on the par-5s. He used a driver only once in 72 holes, at the 16th in the first round.

It meant that on the longer par-4s such as the first, seventh, 12th, 14th, and the 17th, he was surrendering voluntarily as much

as 50 yards to his rivals. To put it another way, he was giving up at least the length of two cricket pitches to Phil Mickelson, Vijay Singh, and Retief Goosen, the three men nearest to him in the Official World Golf Ranking. Nothing altered Woods's thinking, though. He adhered to his plan as rigorously as an iron-fisted Chancellor of the Exchequer sticks to his monetary policy, safe in the knowledge that the quality of his striking with his long and mid irons was so good and so accurate that, even though he was hitting

four and five irons where they were using eight and nine irons, he would not be at a disadvantage.

Nothing demonstrated this so well as his 65 on Friday. While his rivals whaled away with drivers from the tees, Woods hit controlled two and three irons. While they hit eight-iron approaches, Woods used his mid irons that he managed to stop on the greens. It was the round of the Championship, the one that launched him towards victory. He was only in the rough twice. He took 29 putts, holed out from 210 yards for an eagle on the par-4 14th, and dropped only one shot where he took three putts from 75 feet, 15 feet off the putting surface.

All week long, but that day in particular, he played golf by slide rule and compass. He can never have given a better, more consistent demonstration of powerful, accurate, and controlled striking than he did at Hoylake. At Pebble Beach in the 2000 US Open, Woods made such a furious, all-out assault on the course that he left his nearest challenger 15 strokes behind. He has learned such control of his irons, has developed such a vivid imagination for different shots, that the four iron with which he hit a towering approach to the 12th on Friday and then holed out with from over 200 yards on the 14th was the same club he used for a teasing 60-foot chip-and-run from the back of the fifth green.

The abiding memories of Hoylake were of fairways that shone as though they were painted white and laid down between strips of tawny grass and of Woods's thunderous hitting with his irons. If you get the chance to watch Woods in person, stand behind him when he hits a long iron from a tee. The crack of club on ball, the flying divot, the whistle of the ball through the air, and its flight, low and slowly rising, are things that will stay with you forever. So will his play at Hoylake those four days last July.

The Open Championship
Results

Year	Champion	Score	Margin	Runners-up	Venue
1860	Willie Park Snr	174	2	Tom Morris Snr	Prestwick
1861	Tom Morris Snr	163	4	Willie Park Snr	Prestwick
1862	Tom Morris Snr	163	13	Willie Park Snr	Prestwick
1863	Willie Park Snr	168	2	Tom Morris Snr	Prestwick
1864	Tom Morris Snr	167	2	Andrew Strath	Prestwick
1865	Andrew Strath	162	2	Willie Park Snr	Prestwick
1866	Willie Park Snr	169	2	David Park	Prestwick
1867	Tom Morris Snr	170	2	Willie Park Snr	Prestwick
1868	Tom Morris Jnr	154	3	Tom Morris Snr	Prestwick
1869	Tom Morris Jnr	157	11	Bob Kirk	Prestwick
1870	Tom Morris Jnr	149	12	Bob Kirk, David Strath	Prestwick
1871	*No Competition*				
1872	Tom Morris Jnr	166	3	David Strath	Prestwick
1873	Tom Kidd	179	1	Jamie Anderson	St Andrews
1874	Mungo Park	159	2	Tom Morris Jnr	Musselburgh
1875	Willie Park Snr	166	2	Bob Martin	Prestwick
1876	Bob Martin	176	—	David Strath	St Andrews
	(Martin was awarded the title when Strath refused to play-off)				
1877	Jamie Anderson	160	2	Bob Pringle	Musselburgh
1878	Jamie Anderson	157	2	Bob Kirk	Prestwick
1879	Jamie Anderson	169	3	James Allan, Andrew Kirkaldy	St Andrews
1880	Bob Ferguson	162	5	Peter Paxton	Musselburgh
1881	Bob Ferguson	170	3	Jamie Anderson	Prestwick
1882	Bob Ferguson	171	3	Willie Fernie	St Andrews
1883	Willie Fernie	158	Playoff	Bob Ferguson	Musselburgh
1884	Jack Simpson	160	4	Douglas Rolland, Willie Fernie	Prestwick
1885	Bob Martin	171	1	Archie Simpson	St Andrews
1886	David Brown	157	2	Willie Campbell	Musselburgh
1887	Willie Park Jnr	161	1	Bob Martin	Prestwick
1888	Jack Burns	171	1	David Anderson Jnr, Ben Sayers	St Andrews
1889	Willie Park Jnr	155	Playoff	Andrew Kirkaldy	Musselburgh
1890	*John Ball Jnr	164	3	Willie Fernie, Archie Simpson	Prestwick
1891	Hugh Kirkaldy	166	2	Willie Fernie, Andrew Kirkaldy	St Andrews
	(From 1892 the competition was extended to 72 holes)				
1892	*Harold Hilton	305	3	*John Ball Jnr, Hugh Kirkaldy, Sandy Herd	Muirfield

Year	Champion	Score	Margin	Runners-up	Venue
1893	Willie Auchterlonie	322	2	*John Laidlay	Prestwick
1894	J.H. Taylor	326	5	Douglas Rolland	Sandwich
1895	J.H. Taylor	322	4	Sandy Herd	St Andrews
1896	Harry Vardon	316	Playoff	J.H. Taylor	Muirfield
1897	*Harold Hilton	314	1	James Braid	Hoylake
1898	Harry Vardon	307	1	Willie Park Jnr	Prestwick
1899	Harry Vardon	310	5	Jack White	Sandwich
1900	J.H. Taylor	309	8	Harry Vardon	St Andrews
1901	James Braid	309	3	Harry Vardon	Muirfield
1902	Sandy Herd	307	1	Harry Vardon, James Braid	Hoylake
1903	Harry Vardon	300	6	Tom Vardon	Prestwick
1904	Jack White	296	1	James Braid, J.H. Taylor	Sandwich
1905	James Braid	318	5	J.H. Taylor, Rowland Jones	St Andrews
1906	James Braid	300	4	J.H. Taylor	Muirfield
1907	Arnaud Massy	312	2	J.H. Taylor	Hoylake
1908	James Braid	291	8	Tom Ball	Prestwick
1909	J.H. Taylor	295	6	James Braid, Tom Ball	Deal
1910	James Braid	299	4	Sandy Herd	St Andrews
1911	Harry Vardon	303	Playoff	Arnaud Massy	Sandwich
1912	Ted Ray	295	4	Harry Vardon	Muirfield
1913	J.H. Taylor	304	8	Ted Ray	Hoylake
1914	Harry Vardon	306	3	J.H. Taylor	Prestwick
1915-1919 *No Championship*					
1920	George Duncan	303	2	Sandy Herd	Deal
1921	Jock Hutchison	296	Playoff	*Roger Wethered	St Andrews
1922	Walter Hagen	300	1	George Duncan, Jim Barnes	Sandwich
1923	Arthur G. Havers	295	1	Walter Hagen	Troon
1924	Walter Hagen	301	1	Ernest Whitcombe	Hoylake
1925	Jim Barnes	300	1	Archie Compston, Ted Ray	Prestwick
1926	*Robert T. Jones Jnr	291	2	Al Watrous	Royal Lytham
1927	*Robert T. Jones Jnr	285	6	Aubrey Boomer, Fred Robson	St Andrews
1928	Walter Hagen	292	2	Gene Sarazen	Sandwich
1929	Walter Hagen	292	6	John Farrell	Muirfield
1930	*Robert T. Jones Jnr	291	2	Leo Diegel, Macdonald Smith	Hoylake

Gary Player (1959, 1968, 1974), left, and Jack Nicklaus (1966, 1970, 1978) were guests of patrons during The Open.

Todd Hamilton (2004)

Ben Curtis (2003)

David Duval (2001)

Year	Champion	Score	Margin	Runners-up	Venue
1931	Tommy Armour	296	1	Jose Jurado	Carnoustie
1932	Gene Sarazen	283	5	Macdonald Smith	Prince's
1933	Densmore Shute	292	Playoff	Craig Wood	St Andrews
1934	Henry Cotton	283	5	Sid Brews	Sandwich
1935	Alf Perry	283	4	Alf Padgham	Muirfield
1936	Alf Padgham	287	1	Jimmy Adams	Hoylake
1937	Henry Cotton	290	2	Reg Whitcombe	Carnoustie
1938	Reg Whitcombe	295	2	Jimmy Adams	Sandwich
1939	Richard Burton	290	2	Johnny Bulla	St Andrews
1940-1945	*No Championship*				
1946	Sam Snead	290	4	Bobby Locke, Johnny Bulla	St Andrews
1947	Fred Daly	293	1	Reg Horne, *Frank Stranahan	Hoylake
1948	Henry Cotton	284	5	Fred Daly	Muirfield
1949	Bobby Locke	283	Playoff	Harry Bradshaw	Sandwich
1950	Bobby Locke	279	2	Roberto de Vicenzo	Troon
1951	Max Faulkner	285	2	Tony Cerda	Royal Portrush
1952	Bobby Locke	287	1	Peter Thomson	Royal Lytham
1953	Ben Hogan	282	4	*Frank Stranahan, Dai Rees, Peter Thomson, Tony Cerda	Carnoustie
1954	Peter Thomson	283	1	Sid Scott, Dai Rees, Bobby Locke	Royal Birkdale
1955	Peter Thomson	281	2	Johnny Fallon	St Andrews
1956	Peter Thomson	286	3	Flory van Donck	Hoylake
1957	Bobby Locke	279	3	Peter Thomson	St Andrews
1958	Peter Thomson	278	Playoff	David Thomas	Royal Lytham
1959	Gary Player	284	2	Flory van Donck, Fred Bullock	Muirfield
1960	Kel Nagle	278	1	Arnold Palmer	St Andrews
1961	Arnold Palmer	284	1	Dai Rees	Royal Birkdale
1962	Arnold Palmer	276	6	Kel Nagle	Troon
1963	Bob Charles	277	Playoff	Phil Rodgers	Royal Lytham
1964	Tony Lema	279	5	Jack Nicklaus	St Andrews
1965	Peter Thomson	285	2	Christy O'Connor, Brian Huggett	Royal Birkdale
1966	Jack Nicklaus	282	1	David Thomas, Doug Sanders	Muirfield
1967	Roberto de Vicenzo	278	2	Jack Nicklaus	Hoylake
1968	Gary Player	289	2	Jack Nicklaus, Bob Charles	Carnoustie
1969	Tony Jacklin	280	2	Bob Charles	Royal Lytham
1970	Jack Nicklaus	283	Playoff	Doug Sanders	St Andrews

Year	Champion	Score	Margin	Runners-up	Venue
1971	Lee Trevino	278	1	Lu Liang Huan	Royal Birkdale
1972	Lee Trevino	278	1	Jack Nicklaus	Muirfield
1973	Tom Weiskopf	276	3	Neil Coles, Johnny Miller	Troon
1974	Gary Player	282	4	Peter Oosterhuis	Royal Lytham
1975	Tom Watson	279	Playoff	Jack Newton	Carnoustie
1976	Johnny Miller	279	6	Jack Nicklaus, Severiano Ballesteros	Royal Birkdale
1977	Tom Watson	268	1	Jack Nicklaus	Turnberry
1978	Jack Nicklaus	281	2	Simon Owen, Ben Crenshaw, Raymond Floyd, Tom Kite	St Andrews
1979	Severiano Ballesteros	283	3	Jack Nicklaus, Ben Crenshaw	Royal Lytham
1980	Tom Watson	271	4	Lee Trevino	Muirfield
1981	Bill Rogers	276	4	Bernhard Langer	Sandwich
1982	Tom Watson	284	1	Peter Oosterhuis, Nick Price	Royal Troon
1983	Tom Watson	275	1	Hale Irwin, Andy Bean	Royal Birkdale
1984	Severiano Ballesteros	276	2	Bernhard Langer, Tom Watson	St Andrews
1985	Sandy Lyle	282	1	Payne Stewart	Sandwich
1986	Greg Norman	280	5	Gordon J. Brand	Turnberry
1987	Nick Faldo	279	1	Rodger Davis, Paul Azinger	Muirfield
1988	Severiano Ballesteros	273	2	Nick Price	Royal Lytham
1989	Mark Calcavecchia	275	Playoff	Greg Norman, Wayne Grady	Royal Troon
1990	Nick Faldo	270	5	Mark McNulty, Payne Stewart	St Andrews
1991	Ian Baker-Finch	272	2	Mike Harwood	Royal Birkdale
1992	Nick Faldo	272	1	John Cook	Muirfield
1993	Greg Norman	267	2	Nick Faldo	Sandwich
1994	Nick Price	268	1	Jesper Parnevik	Turnberry
1995	John Daly	282	Playoff	Costantino Rocca	St Andrews
1996	Tom Lehman	271	2	Mark McCumber, Ernie Els	Royal Lytham
1997	Justin Leonard	272	3	Jesper Parnevik, Darren Clarke	Royal Troon
1998	Mark O'Meara	280	Playoff	Brian Watts	Royal Birkdale
1999	Paul Lawrie	290	Playoff	Justin Leonard, Jean Van de Velde	Carnoustie
2000	Tiger Woods	269	8	Ernie Els, Thomas Bjorn	St Andrews
2001	David Duval	274	3	Niclas Fasth	Royal Lytham
2002	Ernie Els	278	Playoff	Thomas Levet, Stuart Appleby, Steve Elkington	Muirfield
2003	Ben Curtis	283	1	Thomas Bjorn, Vijay Singh	Sandwich
2004	Todd Hamilton	274	Playoff	Ernie Els	Royal Troon
2005	Tiger Woods	274	5	Colin Montgomerie	St Andrews
2006	Tiger Woods	270	2	Chris DiMarco	Hoylake

*Denotes amateurs

Sandy Lyle (1985)

John Daly (1995)

Tom Lehman (1996)

The Open Championship Records

Most Victories

6, Harry Vardon, 1896-98-99-1903-11-14
5, James Braid, 1901-05-06-08-10; J.H. Taylor, 1894-95-1900-09-13; Peter Thomson, 1954-55-56-58-65; Tom Watson, 1975-77-80-82-83

Most Times Runner-Up or Joint Runner-Up

7, Jack Nicklaus, 1964-67-68-72-76-77-79
6, J.H. Taylor, 1896-1904-05-06-07-14

Oldest Winner

Old Tom Morris, 46 years 99 days, 1867
Harry Vardon, 44 years 41 days, 1914
Roberto de Vicenzo, 44 years 93 days, 1967

Youngest Winner

Young Tom Morris, 17 years 5 months 3 days, 1868
Willie Auchterlonie, 21 years 24 days, 1893
Severiano Ballesteros, 22 years 3 months 12 days, 1979

Youngest and Oldest Competitor

Young Tom Morris, 14 years 4 months 25 days, 1865
Gene Sarazen, 74 years 4 months 9 days, 1976

Biggest Margin of Victory

13 strokes, Old Tom Morris, 1862
12 strokes, Young Tom Morris, 1870
11 strokes, Young Tom Morris, 1869
8 strokes, J.H. Taylor, 1900 and 1913; James Braid, 1908; Tiger Woods, 2000

Lowest Winning Aggregates

267 (66, 68, 69, 64), Greg Norman, Royal St George's, 1993
268 (68, 70, 65, 65), Tom Watson, Turnberry, 1977; (69, 66, 67, 66), Nick Price, Turnberry, 1994
269 (67, 66, 67, 69), Tiger Woods, St Andrews, 2000

Lowest Aggregates in Relation to Par

269 (19 under par), Tiger Woods, St Andrews, 2000
270 (18 under par), Nick Faldo, St Andrews, 1990; Tiger Woods, Hoylake, 2006

Tiger Woods (2000, 2005, 2006)

Lowest Aggregates by Runner-Up

269 (68, 70, 65, 66), Jack Nicklaus, Turnberry, 1977; (69, 63, 70, 67), Nick Faldo, Royal St George's, 1993; (68, 66, 68, 67), Jesper Parnevik, Turnberry, 1994

Lowest Aggregates by an Amateur

281 (68, 72, 70, 71), Iain Pyman, Royal St George's, 1993; (75, 66, 70, 70), Tiger Woods, Royal Lytham, 1996

Lowest Individual Round

63, Mark Hayes, second round, Turnberry, 1977; Isao Aoki, third round, Muirfield, 1980; Greg Norman, second round, Turnberry, 1986; Paul Broadhurst, third round, St Andrews, 1990; Jodie Mudd, fourth round, Royal Birkdale, 1991; Nick Faldo, second round, and Payne Stewart, fourth round, Royal St George's, 1993

Lowest Individual Round by an Amateur

66, Frank Stranahan, fourth round, Troon, 1950; Tiger Woods, second round, Royal Lytham, 1996; Justin Rose, second round, Royal Birkdale, 1998

Tom Watson (1975, 1977, 1980, 1982, 1983)

Lowest First Round

64, Craig Stadler, Royal Birkdale, 1983; Christy O'Connor Jnr., Royal St George's, 1985; Rodger Davis, Muirfield, 1987; Raymond Floyd and Steve Pate, Muirfield, 1992

Lowest Second Round

63, Mark Hayes, Turnberry, 1977; Greg Norman, Turnberry, 1986; Nick Faldo, Royal St George's, 1993

Lowest Third Round

63, Isao Aoki, Muirfield, 1980; Paul Broadhurst, St Andrews, 1990

Lowest Fourth Round

63, Jodie Mudd, Royal Birkdale, 1991; Payne Stewart, Royal St George's, 1993

Lowest First 36 Holes

130 (66, 64), Nick Faldo, Muirfield, 1992

Lowest Second 36 Holes

130 (65, 65), Tom Watson, Turnberry, 1977; (64, 66), Ian Baker-Finch, Royal Birkdale, 1991; (66, 64), Anders Forsbrand, Turnberry, 1994

Lowest Middle 36 Holes

130 (66, 64), Fuzzy Zoeller, Turnberry, 1994

Ernie Els (2002)

Lowest First 54 Holes

198 (67, 67, 64), Tom Lehman, Royal Lytham, 1996
199 (67, 65, 67), Nick Faldo, St Andrews, 1990; (66, 64, 69), Nick Faldo, Muirfield, 1992

Lowest Final 54 Holes

199 (66, 67, 66), Nick Price, Turnberry, 1994

Lowest 9 Holes

28, Denis Durnian, first 9, Royal Birkdale, 1983
29, Peter Thomson and Tom Haliburton, first 9, Royal Lytham, 1958; Tony Jacklin, first 9, St Andrews, 1970; Bill Longmuir, first 9, Royal Lytham, 1979; David J. Russell, first 9, Royal Lytham, 1988; Ian Baker-Finch and Paul Broadhurst, first 9, St Andrews, 1990; Ian Baker-Finch, first 9, Royal Birkdale, 1991; Paul McGinley, first 9, Royal Lytham, 1996; Ernie Els, first 9, Muirfield, 2002; Sergio Garcia, first 9, Royal Liverpool, 2006

Successive Victories

4, Young Tom Morris, 1868-72 (no Championship in 1871).
3, Jamie Anderson, 1877-79; Bob Ferguson, 1880-82, Peter Thomson, 1954-56
2, Old Tom Morris, 1861-62; J.H. Taylor, 1894-95; Harry Vardon, 1898-99; James Braid, 1905-06; Bobby Jones, 1926-27; Walter Hagen, 1928-29; Bobby Locke, 1949-50; Arnold Palmer, 1961-62; Lee Trevino, 1971-72; Tom Watson, 1982-83; Tiger Woods, 2005-06

Victories by Amateurs

3, Bobby Jones, 1926-27-30
2, Harold Hilton, 1892-97
1, John Ball, 1890
Roger Wethered lost a playoff in 1921

Champions in First Appearance

Willie Park, Prestwick, 1860; Tom Kidd, St Andrews, 1873; Mungo Park, Musselburgh, 1874; Harold Hilton, Muirfield, 1892; Jock Hutchison, St Andrews, 1921; Densmore Shute, St Andrews, 1933; Ben Hogan, Carnoustie, 1953; Tony Lema, St Andrews, 1964; Tom Watson, Carnoustie, 1975; Ben Curtis, Sandwich, 2003

Biggest Span Between First and Last Victories

19 years, J.H. Taylor, 1894-1913
18 years, Harry Vardon, 1896-1914
15 years, Gary Player, 1959-74
14 years, Willie Park Snr, 1860-75 (no competition 1871); Henry Cotton, 1934-48

Biggest Span Between Victories

11 years, Henry Cotton, 1937-48

Champions in Three Decades

Harry Vardon, 1896, 1903, 1911
J.H. Taylor, 1894, 1900, 1913
Gary Player, 1959, 1968, 1974

Highest Number of Top-Five Finishes

16, J.H. Taylor, Jack Nicklaus
15, Harry Vardon, James Braid

Highest Number of Rounds Under Par

61, Jack Nicklaus
52, Nick Faldo
42, Tom Watson

Highest Number of Aggregates Under Par

14, Jack Nicklaus, Nick Faldo

Most Consecutive Rounds Under 70

7, Ernie Els, 1993-94

Nick Faldo (1987, 1990, 1992)

Paul Lawrie (1999)   **Mark O'Meara (1998)**

Outright Leader After Every Round

Ted Ray, 1912; Bobby Jones, 1927; Gene Sarazen, 1932; Henry Cotton, 1934; Tom Weiskopf, 1973; Tiger Woods, 2005

Leader After Every Round Including Ties

Harry Vardon, 1899 and 1903; J.H. Taylor, 1900; Lee Trevino, 1971; Gary Player, 1974

Record Leads (Since 1892)

After 18 holes:
4 strokes, James Braid, 1908; Bobby Jones, 1927; Henry Cotton, 1934; Christy O'Connor Jnr., 1985
After 36 holes:
9 strokes, Henry Cotton, 1934
After 54 holes:
10 strokes, Henry Cotton, 1934
7 strokes, Tony Lema, 1964

Biggest Leads by Non-Champions

After 54 holes:
5 strokes, Macdonald Smith, 1925; Jean Van de Velde, 1999

Champions with Each Round Lower Than Previous One

Jack White, 1904, Sandwich, (80, 75, 72, 69)
James Braid, 1906, Muirfield, (77, 76, 74, 73)
Henry Cotton, 1937, Carnoustie, (74, 73, 72, 71)
Ben Hogan, 1953, Carnoustie, (73, 71, 70, 68)
Gary Player, 1959, Muirfield, (75, 71, 70, 68)

Champion with Four Rounds the Same

Densmore Shute, 1933, St Andrews, (73, 73, 73, 73) (excluding the playoff)

Biggest Variation Between Rounds of a Champion

14 strokes, Henry Cotton, 1934, second round 65, fourth round 79
11 strokes, Jack White, 1904, first round 80, fourth round 69; Greg Norman, 1986, first round 74, second round 63, third round 74

Biggest Variation Between Two Rounds

20 strokes, R.G. French, 1938, second round 71, third round 91; Colin Montgomerie, 2002, second round 64, third round 84
19 strokes, R.H. Pemberton, 1938, second round 72, third round 91
18 strokes, A. Tingey Jnr., 1923, first round 94, second round 76
17 strokes, Jack Nicklaus, 1981, first round 83, second round 66; Ian Baker-Finch, 1986, first round 86, second round 69

Best Comeback by Champions

After 18 holes:
Harry Vardon, 1896, 11 strokes behind the leader
After 36 holes:
George Duncan, 1920, 13 strokes behind the leader
After 54 holes:
Paul Lawrie, 1999, 10 strokes behind the leader

Champions with Four Rounds Under 70

Greg Norman, 1993, Royal St George's, (66, 68, 69, 64); Nick Price, 1994, Turnberry, (69, 66, 67, 66); Tiger Woods, 2000, St Andrews, (67, 66, 67, 69)
Of non-champions:
Ernie Els, 1993, Royal St George's, (68, 69, 69, 68); Jesper Parnevik, 1994, Turnberry, (68, 66, 68, 67); Ernie Els, 2004, Royal Troon, (69, 69, 68, 68)

Best Finishing Round by a Champion

64, Greg Norman, Royal St George's, 1993
65, Tom Watson, Turnberry, 1977; Severiano Ballesteros, Royal Lytham, 1988; Justin Leonard, Royal Troon, 1997

Worst Round by a Champion Since 1939

78, Fred Daly, third round, Hoylake, 1947
76, Paul Lawrie, third round, Carnoustie, 1999

Worst Finishing Round by a Champion Since 1939

75, Sam Snead, St Andrews, 1946

Best Opening Round by a Champion

66, Peter Thomson, Royal Lytham, 1958; Nick Faldo, Muirfield, 1992; Greg Norman, Royal St George's, 1993; Tiger Woods, St Andrews, 2005

Biggest Recovery in 18 Holes by a Champion

George Duncan, Deal, 1920, was 13 strokes behind the leader, Abe Mitchell, after 36 holes and level after 54

Most Appearances

46, Gary Player
38, Jack Nicklaus

Mark Calcavecchia (1989)

Most Appearances on Final Day (Since 1892)

32, Jack Nicklaus
31, Alex Herd
30, J.H. Taylor
27, Harry Vardon, James Braid, Nick Faldo
26, Peter Thomson, Gary Player
23, Dai Rees
22, Henry Cotton

Most Appearances Before First Victory

16, Nick Price, 1994
14, Mark O'Meara, 1998

Most Appearances Without a Victory

29, Dai Rees
28, Sam Torrance
27, Neil Coles

Championship with Highest Number of Rounds Under 70

148, Turnberry, 1994

Championship Since 1946 with the Fewest Rounds Under 70

St Andrews, 1946; Hoylake, 1947; Portrush, 1951; Hoylake, 1956; Carnoustie, 1968. All had only two rounds under 70.

Longest Course

Carnoustie, 1999, 7361 yards

Courses Most Often Used

St Andrews, 27; Prestwick, 24; Muirfield, 15; Sandwich, 13; Hoylake, 11; Royal Lytham, 10; Royal Birkdale and Royal Troon, 8; Musselburgh and Carnoustie, 6; Turnberry, 3; Deal, 2; Royal Portrush and Prince's, 1

Prize Money

Year	Total	First Prize
1860	nil	nil
1863	10	nil
1864	15	6
1876	27	10
1889	22	8
1891	30.50	10
1892	100	35
1893	100	30
1910	135	50
1920	225	75
1927	275	75
1930	400	100
1931	500	100
1946	1,000	150
1949	1,500	300
1953	2,500	500
1954	3,500	750
1955	3,750	1,000
1958	4,850	1,000
1959	5,000	1,000
1960	7,000	1,250
1961	8,500	1,400
1963	8,500	1,500
1965	10,000	1,750
1966	15,000	2,100
1968	20,000	3,000
1969	30,334	4,250
1970	40,000	5,250
1971	45,000	5,500
1972	50,000	5,500
1975	75,000	7,500
1977	100,000	10,000
1978	125,000	12,500
1979	155,000	15,000
1980	200,000	25,000
1982	250,000	32,000
1983	310,000	40,000
1984	445,000	50,000
1985	530,000	65,000
1986	634,000	70,000
1987	650,000	75,000
1988	700,000	80,000
1989	750,000	80,000
1990	825,000	85,000

Year	Total	First Prize
1991	900,000	90,000
1992	950,000	95,000
1993	1,000,000	100,000
1994	1,100,000	110,000
1995	1,250,000	125,000
1996	1,400,000	200,000
1997	1,586,300	250,000
1998	1,800,000	300,000
1999	2,000,000	350,000

Year	Total	First Prize
2000	2,750,000	500,000
2001	3,300,000	600,000
2002	3,800,000	700,000
2003	3,900,000	700,000
2004	4,000,000	720,000
2005	4,000,000	720,000
2006	4,000,000	720,000

Attendance

Year	Total	Year	Total	Year	Total
1962	37,098	1977	87,615	1992	146,427
1963	24,585	1978	125,271	1993	141,000
1964	35,954	1979	134,501	1994	128,000
1965	32,927	1980	131,610	1995	180,000
1966	40,182	1981	111,987	1996	170,000
1967	29,880	1982	133,299	1997	176,000
1968	51,819	1983	142,892	1998	195,100
1969	46,001	1984	193,126	1999	157,000
1970	81,593	1985	141,619	2000	238,787
1971	70,076	1986	134,261	2001	178,000
1972	84,746	1987	139,189	2002	161,500
1973	78,810	1988	191,334	2003	183,000
1974	92,796	1989	160,639	2004	176,000
1975	85,258	1990	208,680	2005	223,000
1976	92,021	1991	189,435	2006	230,000

The 135th Open Championship

Complete Scores
Courtesy of Unisys

HOLE			1	2	3	4	5	6	7	8	9	10	11	12	13	14	15	16	17	18	
PAR	POSITION		4	4	4	4	5	3	4	4	3	5	4	4	3	4	3	5	4	5	TOTAL
Tiger Woods	T2	Round 1	5	4	4	4	4	3	4	4	2	5	3	4	3	4	3	4	4	3	67
USA	1	Round 2	4	4	5	3	4	3	4	3	3	4	3	4	3	2	3	4	4	5	65
£720,000	1	Round 3	4	5	4	4	4	2	5	4	3	5	3	4	3	5	3	4	5	4	71
	1	Round 4	4	4	4	4	3	3	4	4	3	4	4	5	3	3	2	4	4	5	**67 -270**
Chris DiMarco	T33	Round 1	4	3	3	3	5	3	7	4	3	4	4	5	3	4	2	4	5	4	70
USA	3	Round 2	3	3	4	4	5	3	4	3	2	4	3	4	3	4	2	5	5	4	65
£430,000	T2	Round 3	4	4	3	4	5	3	5	4	4	5	3	3	2	4	3	4	4	5	69
	2	Round 4	5	4	4	4	5	2	4	4	3	4	4	4	2	4	3	4	4	4	**68 -272**
Ernie Els	T7	Round 1	5	3	3	4	5	3	4	4	3	4	5	4	2	3	3	4	4	5	68
South Africa	2	Round 2	4	4	3	4	4	2	4	3	4	4	4	4	3	3	3	4	4	4	65
£275,000	T2	Round 3	5	3	4	4	5	3	5	4	2	5	4	4	4	4	3	4	4	4	71
	3	Round 4	4	4	4	4	4	3	4	5	3	5	5	4	3	3	3	4	4	5	**71 -275**
Jim Furyk	T7	Round 1	4	5	3	4	4	3	4	3	3	4	4	4	3	5	3	4	4	4	68
USA	T9	Round 2	4	5	4	4	5	3	5	4	2	4	4	4	2	4	3	5	4	5	71
£210,000	T5	Round 3	4	3	4	4	4	2	3	4	3	4	3	5	3	5	3	4	3	5	66
	4	Round 4	5	5	4	4	5	3	5	4	3	4	4	4	3	4	2	4	4	4	**71 -276**
Hideto Tanihara	T68	Round 1	4	5	3	3	5	3	3	4	3	5	5	5	3	5	2	4	4	6	72
Japan	T22	Round 2	4	4	3	3	4	3	4	5	3	4	4	6	2	4	3	4	4	4	68
£159,500	7	Round 3	4	4	4	4	4	2	5	3	4	4	4	4	3	4	2	4	4	4	66
	T5	Round 4	4	3	4	4	6	5	4	4	2	5	4	3	3	3	3	4	5	5	**71 -277**
Sergio Garcia	T7	Round 1	3	4	4	4	4	3	3	4	3	5	4	4	3	5	3	4	4	4	68
Spain	T9	Round 2	3	4	4	4	4	3	3	4	3	5	4	5	4	4	3	5	4	5	71
£159,500	T2	Round 3	4	2	4	4	4	3	3	3	2	5	4	4	3	4	3	5	4	4	65
	T5	Round 4	4	5	5	4	5	3	4	5	4	5	5	3	3	5	2	3	4	5	**73 -277**
Angel Cabrera	T50	Round 1	4	5	4	4	4	3	5	4	3	4	3	4	3	4	3	6	3	5	71
Argentina	T9	Round 2	3	4	4	4	4	3	3	4	3	4	4	4	3	4	3	6	4	4	68
£128,000	T5	Round 3	5	4	4	3	4	3	4	4	3	4	4	3	4	3	2	3	4	5	66
	7	Round 4	4	7	4	4	4	3	4	4	3	4	4	5	4	4	3	4	4	4	**73 -278**
Carl Pettersson	T7	Round 1	4	6	4	4	4	3	4	5	3	4	3	4	3	4	2	4	3	4	68
Sweden	T22	Round 2	4	5	4	4	5	4	4	4	3	4	4	5	3	4	2	4	4	5	72
£95,333	T16	Round 3	4	4	5	4	3	3	5	5	3	4	4	4	3	5	3	4	5	4	70
	T8	Round 4	5	4	6	4	4	3	3	4	3	3	4	4	3	5	2	4	4	4	**69 -279**

* Denotes amateurs

HOLE			1	2	3	4	5	6	7	8	9	10	11	12	13	14	15	16	17	18	
PAR	POSITION		4	4	4	4	5	3	4	4	3	5	4	4	3	4	3	5	4	5	TOTAL
Andres Romero	T33	Round 1	4	4	4	3	5	4	4	4	3	4	5	4	3	4	3	4	4	4	70
Argentina	T22	Round 2	3	4	4	4	4	3	4	4	3	5	4	4	4	4	3	5	4	4	70
£95,333	T10	Round 3	4	4	5	3	4	3	3	4	3	4	3	5	3	3	3	5	4	5	68
	T8	Round 4	4	4	4	3	4	2	4	4	4	5	3	4	4	5	3	4	5	5	71 **-279**
Adam Scott	T7	Round 1	4	3	5	4	4	3	4	3	3	6	3	4	2	4	3	3	5	5	68
Australia	T5	Round 2	4	5	4	3	4	3	5	4	3	4	3	4	3	4	3	5	4	4	69
£95,333	T8	Round 3	4	5	4	5	4	3	3	4	3	4	4	4	3	4	3	4	4	5	70
	T8	Round 4	5	5	3	4	4	3	4	4	2	4	5	4	3	4	2	4	5	7	72 **-279**
Anthony Wall	T2	Round 1	4	4	4	4	4	3	3	4	3	3	5	4	2	4	3	3	5	5	67
England	T22	Round 2	5	3	5	4	5	3	4	4	3	5	3	4	3	4	4	4	4	6	73
£69,333	T25	Round 3	4	4	5	4	4	3	5	4	3	5	4	4	2	4	3	3	4	6	71
	T11	Round 4	4	4	3	4	5	3	3	4	3	4	4	4	3	4	3	5	5	4	69 **-280**
Ben Crane	T7	Round 1	5	4	4	3	4	3	4	4	3	4	4	4	2	4	4	4	4	4	68
USA	T9	Round 2	4	5	4	5	4	3	4	3	3	5	5	4	3	4	3	3	4	5	71
£69,333	T16	Round 3	4	4	4	3	4	3	5	4	3	5	4	5	3	6	3	3	4	4	71
	T11	Round 4	4	4	4	3	5	4	4	4	3	5	4	4	3	4	2	4	4	5	70 **-280**
S K Ho	T7	Round 1	4	3	4	4	4	3	4	3	3	4	4	4	3	5	3	4	4	5	68
South Korea	T37	Round 2	5	4	3	4	5	3	4	4	4	4	4	3	3	5	3	6	4	5	73
£69,333	T16	Round 3	4	4	4	4	3	3	4	4	3	4	4	4	3	4	3	4	5	5	69
	T11	Round 4	4	4	4	4	4	3	4	4	2	4	5	4	4	4	3	4	5	4	70 **-280**
Sean O'Hair	T20	Round 1	4	3	4	4	3	4	4	4	2	5	4	4	3	5	2	4	6	4	69
USA	T42	Round 2	5	5	5	4	3	3	6	4	3	5	4	4	3	3	4	4	4	4	73
£56,500	T48	Round 3	3	4	4	5	5	3	4	3	4	4	4	3	7	3	5	4	4	3	72
	T14	Round 4	4	4	4	4	4	3	4	4	2	4	4	3	5	3	4	3	4	4	67 **-281**
Retief Goosen	T33	Round 1	3	5	4	4	4	3	4	3	3	4	4	4	2	5	4	5	4	5	70
South Africa	4	Round 2	4	4	3	4	3	3	4	3	3	4	4	4	3	4	4	3	5	4	66
£56,500	T10	Round 3	4	4	3	5	6	4	3	4	3	4	4	5	3	3	5	5	4	3	72
	T14	Round 4	4	5	4	4	5	4	4	4	3	4	4	5	3	5	2	4	4	5	73 **-281**
Robert Rock	T20	Round 1	3	4	4	4	4	2	4	4	4	5	3	5	3	5	2	5	4	4	69
England	8	Round 2	4	5	5	5	4	3	4	4	3	3	3	4	3	4	2	5	4	4	69
£45,000	T25	Round 3	4	6	5	4	5	2	4	5	3	4	4	4	2	5	3	4	4	5	73
	T16	Round 4	3	4	5	3	5	3	4	4	2	5	4	5	4	4	3	5	4	4	71 **-282**
Brett Rumford	T7	Round 1	3	5	4	3	3	3	4	4	3	4	4	4	4	3	4	4	4	5	68
Australia	T9	Round 2	4	4	5	3	4	3	4	4	4	5	4	4	3	5	3	4	4	4	71
£45,000	T25	Round 3	4	4	5	4	3	3	5	4	3	4	3	5	4	4	3	4	5	5	72
	T16	Round 4	5	5	4	4	4	3	3	4	3	3	5	5	3	5	3	4	4	4	71 **-282**
Mikko Ilonen	T7	Round 1	4	4	4	4	5	2	4	3	3	4	4	4	3	4	3	4	5	4	68
Finland	T5	Round 2	4	6	3	4	4	3	4	4	3	4	3	4	3	4	2	5	4	5	69
£45,000	T16	Round 3	4	5	4	3	5	3	4	3	2	5	4	5	3	5	4	5	4	5	73
	T16	Round 4	4	5	3	5	4	3	6	4	3	4	4	4	3	4	2	5	4	5	72 **-282**
Geoff Ogilvy	T50	Round 1	4	4	5	4	5	3	4	3	3	4	4	4	4	3	5	4	4	4	71
Australia	T22	Round 2	4	4	4	4	4	3	3	4	3	7	4	3	3	5	2	4	3	5	69
£45,000	T16	Round 3	4	4	3	4	4	3	5	4	3	4	4	4	4	3	4	4	5	4	70
	T16	Round 4	4	4	4	4	4	4	4	4	3	5	4	5	3	4	3	4	5	4	72 **-282**
Robert Allenby	T20	Round 1	4	4	4	4	4	3	4	4	3	4	4	2	4	3	5	5	4	4	69
Australia	T9	Round 2	5	4	4	4	5	3	4	4	2	4	4	3	4	5	3	4	4	4	70
£45,000	T10	Round 3	5	4	4	4	5	3	4	4	2	4	4	3	4	4	3	4	4	4	69
	T16	Round 4	6	4	4	4	5	3	4	4	2	6	4	4	3	3	4	6	4	4	74 **-282**

HOLE			1	2	3	4	5	6	7	8	9	10	11	12	13	14	15	16	17	18	
PAR	POSITION		4	4	4	4	5	3	4	4	3	5	4	4	3	4	3	5	4	5	TOTAL
Peter Lonard	T50	Round 1	5	4	6	4	4	3	3	4	3	4	4	4	4	4	2	4	5	4	71
Australia	T22	Round 2	4	5	5	4	4	3	5	4	4	4	3	4	2	4	2	4	4	4	69
£45,000	T10	Round 3	3	5	3	4	5	3	4	3	3	4	4	4	3	4	3	4	4	5	68
	T16	Round 4	4	5	4	4	4	3	4	4	3	5	4	4	3	4	3	5	5	6	74 -282
Mark Hensby	T7	Round 1	4	4	7	3	4	3	4	3	2	4	3	5	3	3	3	4	5	4	68
Australia	T22	Round 2	4	4	4	5	4	4	4	4	3	4	3	4	3	4	3	6	4	5	72
£35,375	T48	Round 3	5	4	4	3	4	4	5	3	3	6	3	5	4	5	3	6	4	3	74
	T22	Round 4	4	4	4	4	4	2	5	4	3	5	4	4	3	3	3	5	5	3	69 -283
Phil Mickelson	T20	Round 1	3	5	4	4	3	3	3	4	3	4	4	5	3	5	3	4	4	5	69
USA	T22	Round 2	4	4	4	4	5	2	5	4	3	4	4	4	3	5	3	4	4	5	71
£35,375	T39	Round 3	4	4	4	4	5	3	5	5	4	5	4	4	3	5	3	4	4	3	73
	T22	Round 4	3	4	4	4	4	3	5	4	2	4	3	5	3	5	4	4	4	5	70 -283
Charl Schwartzel	T108	Round 1	4	4	4	4	5	3	4	4	4	5	4	4	3	4	3	5	4	6	74
South Africa	T22	Round 2	4	4	4	4	4	3	5	4	3	4	4	3	3	3	2	4	4	4	66
£35,375	T33	Round 3	3	5	5	4	5	3	4	4	3	4	4	4	3	5	4	4	4	4	72
	T22	Round 4	4	4	4	4	6	4	3	4	3	4	3	5	3	5	3	4	4	4	71 -283
Greg Owen	T2	Round 1	4	4	4	4	4	3	4	3	3	5	4	5	2	3	3	4	4	4	67
England	T22	Round 2	5	4	4	4	4	2	3	4	2	5	4	5	4	4	3	5	4	7	73
£35,375	T10	Round 3	4	5	4	3	4	3	4	4	3	4	4	3	4	3	5	3	4	4	68
	T22	Round 4	4	4	5	4	5	4	5	5	3	4	4	4	4	4	3	5	4	4	75 -283
Paul Broadhurst	T50	Round 1	4	4	4	4	4	4	3	5	4	4	4	4	3	4	3	4	5	4	71
England	T48	Round 2	5	5	5	4	3	3	3	3	3	5	5	4	3	4	3	4	4	5	71
£29,100	T51	Round 3	4	5	4	4	4	3	5	4	3	5	4	4	3	4	3	4	5	5	73
	T26	Round 4	3	5	4	4	3	3	3	4	3	3	6	4	3	6	3	4	4	4	69 -284
Rory Sabbatini	T20	Round 1	5	4	4	4	4	3	3	4	3	3	4	5	3	4	3	5	3	5	69
South Africa	T9	Round 2	5	5	4	4	5	3	3	4	3	5	3	3	2	4	3	4	5	5	70
£29,100	T33	Round 3	4	4	4	5	4	3	4	4	3	6	4	5	3	4	4	4	4	4	73
	T26	Round 4	4	5	4	3	5	3	4	4	3	6	4	4	3	3	4	5	4	4	72 -284
Lee Slattery	T20	Round 1	4	4	4	4	4	3	4	3	4	4	4	4	3	5	3	4	4	5	69
England	T37	Round 2	4	4	4	3	5	3	4	5	3	4	4	5	3	5	3	4	4	5	72
£29,100	T33	Round 3	4	4	4	4	3	3	5	4	3	4	4	4	2	6	3	5	4	4	71
	T26	Round 4	4	5	4	4	4	4	5	4	3	4	4	4	3	4	3	4	4	5	72 -284
Hunter Mahan	T92	Round 1	4	4	5	4	4	3	5	4	3	4	4	4	4	5	3	4	5	4	73
USA	T57	Round 2	4	4	5	5	5	3	4	4	2	4	4	4	3	3	3	5	3	5	70
£29,100	T25	Round 3	4	4	4	4	4	2	3	4	3	4	4	4	3	5	3	5	4	4	68
	T26	Round 4	4	5	4	5	4	5	4	4	3	5	4	4	3	3	2	4	5	5	73 -284
Jerry Kelly	T68	Round 1	5	4	4	4	5	3	4	4	3	4	4	4	3	5	3	4	5	4	72
USA	T9	Round 2	3	4	4	4	3	4	5	4	4	4	4	4	3	4	3	3	4	4	67
£29,100	T10	Round 3	4	4	4	3	5	4	3	4	3	4	4	4	3	4	3	5	4	4	69
	T26	Round 4	4	5	4	4	5	5	4	3	2	4	4	4	3	6	4	6	5	4	76 -284
Lee Westwood	T20	Round 1	4	3	5	5	4	3	4	4	2	4	4	5	3	4	3	4	4	4	69
England	T37	Round 2	4	4	4	4	6	3	4	4	3	5	4	4	3	4	3	4	4	5	72
£24,500	T54	Round 3	4	5	5	6	4	3	4	4	3	4	4	4	4	4	4	4	4	5	75
	T31	Round 4	4	5	4	4	4	3	4	4	3	5	4	3	3	5	2	4	4	4	69 -285
Thaworn Wiratchant	T50	Round 1	4	3	5	3	5	3	4	3	3	5	5	5	3	4	3	4	4	5	71
Thailand	T9	Round 2	4	4	3	4	4	3	4	4	3	4	4	5	3	4	3	4	4	4	68
£24,500	T39	Round 3	4	2	4	4	4	3	4	5	3	4	4	6	4	5	3	6	5	4	74
	T31	Round 4	4	4	4	4	4	3	4	4	2	5	4	3	4	4	4	4	5	6	72 -285

HOLE		1	2	3	4	5	6	7	8	9	10	11	12	13	14	15	16	17	18	
PAR	**POSITION**	4	4	4	4	5	3	4	4	3	5	4	4	3	4	3	5	4	5	**TOTAL**
Simon Khan	T33 Round 1	3	4	4	3	5	3	4	3	4	5	4	4	3	5	3	4	5	4	70
England	T48 Round 2	4	4	4	5	4	3	4	4	3	5	4	4	3	3	3	6	5	4	72
£24,500	T16 Round 3	4	3	5	4	4	3	4	4	4	3	3	5	3	5	3	3	4	4	68
	T31 Round 4	5	5	4	4	6	4	4	4	3	5	4	4	3	4	3	4	4	5	75 **-285**
Scott Verplank	T33 Round 1	4	5	4	4	4	3	4	4	3	4	4	5	3	4	3	4	4	4	70
USA	T57 Round 2	4	5	4	4	4	3	4	4	3	4	4	5	3	5	3	4	5	5	73
£24,500	T16 Round 3	3	4	4	3	4	3	4	2	5	3	4	3	4	3	4	4	5	5	67
	T31 Round 4	4	4	4	5	5	4	4	6	2	4	3	4	3	4	4	5	5	5	75 **-285**
Michael Campbell	T33 Round 1	4	4	4	4	3	5	3	3	5	4	4	2	4	3	5	4	4	5	70
New Zealand	T37 Round 2	4	4	4	4	5	3	4	4	3	5	4	4	3	5	3	4	4	4	71
£19,625	T54 Round 3	4	5	4	5	6	4	4	4	3	4	4	4	3	5	4	4	4	4	75
	T35 Round 4	4	4	4	4	5	2	4	4	3	3	4	5	3	5	3	4	4	5	70 **-286**
John Senden	T33 Round 1	5	4	4	4	4	3	4	4	2	5	4	4	3	4	3	5	3	5	70
Australia	T57 Round 2	6	5	4	4	4	3	5	3	3	6	5	4	3	4	3	4	3	4	73
£19,625	T54 Round 3	4	4	4	4	5	3	4	4	2	4	7	4	1	4	3	5	4	7	73
	T35 Round 4	4	4	4	4	4	5	4	5	3	4	3	4	2	5	3	4	4	4	70 **-286**
Luke Donald	T108 Round 1	4	4	5	4	6	3	3	5	3	4	4	4	3	5	3	4	5	5	74
England	T48 Round 2	4	3	4	5	4	3	3	4	2	4	3	5	4	4	3	3	5	5	68
£19,625	T51 Round 3	5	4	4	4	5	3	5	3	3	5	3	4	4	4	3	5	4	5	73
	T35 Round 4	4	4	4	4	4	3	4	3	3	6	4	3	4	3	5	4	5	71	71 **-286**
Rod Pampling	T20 Round 1	4	5	4	4	5	4	4	3	4	4	4	3	4	3	4	4	4	3	69
Australia	T22 Round 2	4	4	5	4	4	3	4	5	4	4	4	5	3	4	2	4	4	4	71
£19,625	T48 Round 3	4	5	4	4	4	3	4	4	3	5	4	4	3	6	3	5	4	5	74
	T35 Round 4	4	4	4	4	5	5	4	5	3	4	4	4	3	4	2	4	4	5	72 **-286**
Robert Karlsson	T33 Round 1	4	4	4	4	4	4	4	4	3	4	5	5	2	4	3	3	4	5	70
Sweden	T37 Round 2	4	4	4	4	4	4	4	4	3	4	4	4	3	4	3	5	4	5	71
£19,625	T33 Round 3	5	4	4	5	4	3	5	3	3	4	4	5	3	4	3	3	5	4	71
	T35 Round 4	5	4	4	4	5	5	4	3	4	4	4	4	4	5	3	4	4	4	74 **-286**
Marcus Fraser	T7 Round 1	4	4	4	4	4	3	4	4	2	4	4	4	2	5	3	4	5	4	68
Australia	T9 Round 2	4	5	4	3	6	2	4	4	3	5	4	4	3	5	3	4	4	4	71
£19,625	T25 Round 3	4	3	4	4	5	3	5	4	3	4	4	4	5	2	5	5	4	72	72
	T35 Round 4	4	4	5	4	5	3	4	4	3	5	4	5	3	4	2	6	5	5	75 **-286**
Thomas Bjorn	T68 Round 1	4	4	4	4	5	2	5	4	4	4	5	4	3	4	3	4	4	5	72
Denmark	T57 Round 2	4	5	4	4	6	2	4	4	3	4	3	4	3	5	3	4	4	5	71
£14,857	T54 Round 3	4	4	4	4	5	4	4	4	3	4	4	5	3	4	3	4	5	5	73
	T41 Round 4	4	4	4	4	5	3	5	4	3	4	4	4	2	5	3	4	5	4	71 **-287**
Brandt Jobe	T20 Round 1	4	5	3	3	4	3	3	4	3	4	4	4	4	4	3	4	5	5	69
USA	T22 Round 2	4	4	4	4	4	3	4	4	3	5	4	4	3	5	3	4	4	5	71
£14,857	T51 Round 3	3	5	4	5	5	3	4	4	3	4	5	4	4	3	3	5	5	5	75
	T41 Round 4	5	4	4	5	4	3	4	3	2	4	4	5	4	5	3	5	4	4	72 **-287**
Miguel A Jimenez	T2 Round 1	4	4	4	5	4	3	4	3	2	4	4	4	3	4	3	4	4	4	67
Spain	T5 Round 2	3	4	4	3	3	3	5	5	3	5	5	4	3	4	3	5	4	4	70
£14,857	T39 Round 3	4	4	4	4	4	4	6	4	2	5	4	4	4	4	3	5	5	6	76
	T41 Round 4	4	5	4	4	5	4	3	4	3	5	5	5	4	5	2	4	4	4	74 **-287**
Stephen Ames	T33 Round 1	4	5	4	4	5	3	5	4	3	3	4	4	3	4	3	4	4	4	70
Canada	T37 Round 2	4	4	4	4	5	2	4	4	3	5	5	4	3	4	3	5	5	3	71
£14,857	T39 Round 3	4	4	4	5	5	3	5	4	3	4	3	4	4	4	3	5	4	4	72
	T41 Round 4	4	5	3	4	6	2	5	4	3	4	4	4	3	5	3	4	5	6	74 **-287**

HOLE			1	2	3	4	5	6	7	8	9	10	11	12	13	14	15	16	17	18	
PAR	POSITION		4	4	4	4	5	3	4	4	3	5	4	4	3	4	3	5	4	5	TOTAL
Soren Kjeldsen	T50	Round 1	5	4	5	4	5	3	4	4	3	4	3	5	3	4	3	4	4	4	71
Denmark	T48	Round 2	4	4	4	4	3	4	4	4	3	5	4	4	4	4	3	4	4	5	71
£14,857	T39	Round 3	5	4	3	4	4	3	5	4	3	4	4	5	3	5	2	4	3	6	71
	T41	Round 4	4	5	5	4	6	3	4	4	3	4	4	4	3	4	3	3	5	6	74 -287
Jeff Sluman	T50	Round 1	4	4	3	4	4	3	4	5	3	5	4	5	4	4	3	4	4	4	71
USA	T57	Round 2	4	5	3	4	4	3	4	4	3	5	4	5	3	4	3	5	4	5	72
£14,857	T25	Round 3	4	3	4	4	5	2	4	4	3	4	4	5	4	4	2	4	4	4	68
	T41	Round 4	5	4	4	4	4	2	5	6	3	5	5	5	3	5	3	4	4	5	76 -287
Mark Calcavecchia	T50	Round 1	3	4	4	4	4	3	4	4	3	4	4	4	3	5	3	6	4	5	71
USA	T9	Round 2	4	4	3	4	4	2	4	5	3	3	4	5	4	3	2	6	4	4	68
£14,857	T8	Round 3	3	4	4	3	4	3	5	4	3	4	3	5	3	4	2	5	5	4	68
	T41	Round 4	4	5	4	4	5	4	4	4	3	5	5	6	3	4	3	6	4	7	80 -287
*Marius Thorp	T50	Round 1	3	3	4	4	5	3	6	4	2	4	4	6	4	4	3	4	4	4	71
Norway	T48	Round 2	5	4	4	4	5	4	4	4	3	4	4	4	2	4	2	5	5	4	71
	T58	Round 3	4	5	4	5	5	3	4	4	3	4	5	4	2	5	3	6	4	5	75
	T48	Round 4	5	4	4	4	5	3	4	4	3	5	3	3	3	4	3	5	5	4	71 -288
Tom Watson	T68	Round 1	4	4	4	4	6	3	4	4	3	4	3	4	4	4	3	4	5	5	72
USA	T48	Round 2	4	5	3	4	4	3	4	3	2	5	4	4	2	4	3	6	6	4	70
£11,607	T58	Round 3	6	4	3	3	4	3	4	4	3	5	5	4	4	5	3	4	5	6	75
	T48	Round 4	4	4	4	4	4	4	4	5	3	4	4	4	4	4	2	4	4	5	71 -288
Henrik Stenson	T68	Round 1	4	4	5	4	5	3	5	4	3	3	4	5	3	4	4	4	4	4	72
Sweden	T57	Round 2	3	5	4	5	4	3	4	4	3	5	3	4	3	4	4	4	4	5	71
£11,607	T58	Round 3	3	4	4	4	4	3	4	3	3	4	4	5	3	4	3	9	6	4	74
	T48	Round 4	3	4	4	4	4	3	5	4	5	5	4	4	2	3	3	5	4	5	71 -288
Simon Dyson	T108	Round 1	4	4	4	4	5	3	5	4	3	5	5	4	3	4	5	4	4	4	74
England	T57	Round 2	3	5	3	4	3	3	4	5	3	4	3	5	3	5	2	4	4	6	69
£11,607	T39	Round 3	4	5	4	3	4	4	4	4	4	4	4	3	3	3	3	4	4	6	70
	T48	Round 4	4	5	6	4	4	3	4	5	2	5	3	7	3	4	3	4	4	5	75 -288
Simon Wakefield	T68	Round 1	4	4	5	5	4	4	4	3	3	5	4	5	2	4	3	5	4	4	72
England	T57	Round 2	4	3	4	4	4	3	3	5	3	5	4	5	3	5	3	4	4	5	71
£11,607	T39	Round 3	4	5	4	4	5	4	4	3	4	4	4	4	3	4	3	4	4	4	70
	T48	Round 4	4	6	4	4	6	4	4	4	4	5	4	4	4	3	2	4	4	5	75 -288
G Fernandez-Castano	T33	Round 1	4	4	5	4	5	3	5	4	2	4	4	4	3	4	3	4	4	4	70
Spain	T9	Round 2	4	4	4	4	5	3	4	5	3	3	4	4	3	5	2	4	4	4	69
£11,607	T33	Round 3	4	3	6	5	5	4	4	4	4	4	3	3	3	4	3	5	4	5	73
	T48	Round 4	4	5	4	4	5	4	5	4	3	5	4	5	2	4	3	6	5	4	76 -288
John Bickerton	T68	Round 1	5	5	3	4	7	3	4	4	2	5	4	5	3	4	3	3	4	4	72
England	T48	Round 2	4	4	4	4	6	3	4	4	4	4	4	4	3	4	2	4	3	5	70
£11,607	T33	Round 3	3	4	4	5	5	3	4	5	3	4	4	5	3	4	3	4	3	4	70
	T48	Round 4	4	5	4	4	5	3	6	5	3	5	4	4	3	5	2	5	4	5	76 -288
Andrew Marshall	T68	Round 1	4	5	4	4	5	4	4	4	3	4	4	4	4	4	2	4	4	5	72
England	T57	Round 2	4	4	4	4	4	3	5	3	3	6	4	4	3	5	3	4	4	4	71
£11,607	T25	Round 3	4	4	4	3	4	3	4	4	3	4	3	5	3	5	3	4	4	4	68
	T48	Round 4	6	4	4	4	5	4	5	4	3	4	4	4	3	4	4	5	5	5	77 -288
David Duval	T33	Round 1	4	4	4	4	5	4	4	4	2	3	4	4	3	5	3	5	4	4	70
USA	T22	Round 2	4	4	6	4	5	3	4	4	2	4	4	4	3	4	2	5	4	4	70
£10,300	T64	Round 3	5	4	5	4	5	4	6	5	3	5	5	4	3	5	4	3	4	4	78
	T56	Round 4	5	4	4	4	4	3	4	4	4	4	4	4	3	4	3	3	5	5	71 -289

			1	2	3	4	5	6	7	8	9	10	11	12	13	14	15	16	17	18	
PAR	POSITION		4	4	4	4	5	3	4	4	3	5	4	4	3	4	3	5	4	5	TOTAL
Jose M Olazabal	T92	Round 1	4	5	4	4	6	4	4	4	2	5	4	4	3	5	3	4	4	4	73
Spain	T37	Round 2	4	4	3	4	5	3	5	4	2	4	4	4	3	4	2	4	4	5	68
£10,300	T58	Round 3	4	4	5	5	4	3	4	5	3	4	7	5	3	4	3	4	5	4	76
	T56	Round 4	4	5	4	4	5	3	4	4	3	5	5	4	3	3	3	4	4	5	72 -**289**
Mike Weir	T7	Round 1	5	3	5	3	4	3	4	4	3	4	4	4	2	4	3	4	4	5	68
Canada	T22	Round 2	5	4	4	4	5	3	3	4	3	4	4	4	4	4	3	4	6	4	72
£10,300	T39	Round 3	3	4	4	4	4	4	4	3	3	4	4	5	3	5	3	5	5	6	73
	T56	Round 4	4	4	5	4	4	4	4	3	2	5	4	6	4	3	3	7	6	4	76 -**289**
Keiichiro Fukabori	T2	Round 1	5	4	4	4	4	2	4	3	3	4	4	4	2	5	2	4	5	4	67
Japan	T22	Round 2	4	4	4	4	5	3	4	5	3	5	5	4	3	4	3	4	5	4	73
£10,300	T16	Round 3	5	4	5	4	4	3	4	4	4	4	3	4	2	4	3	4	4	5	70
	T56	Round 4	4	4	4	4	5	5	4	4	3	5	6	5	5	4	4	5	4	4	79 -**289**
Tim Clark	T68	Round 1	4	4	4	4	4	3	4	4	3	4	5	4	3	5	3	5	5	4	72
South Africa	T37	Round 2	5	3	4	4	5	2	5	4	3	4	4	4	3	4	3	4	4	4	69
£10,300	T16	Round 3	5	4	4	3	5	2	3	4	3	5	4	5	3	3	2	5	5	4	69
	T56	Round 4	5	5	4	4	6	3	4	4	3	4	5	4	3	6	3	5	6	5	79 -**289**
Andrew Buckle	T68	Round 1	5	5	4	4	4	3	4	4	4	4	3	4	3	4	3	4	5	5	72
Australia	T37	Round 2	5	4	4	3	4	2	4	3	3	5	5	4	3	4	3	4	4	5	69
£9,950	T39	Round 3	4	4	4	4	4	4	4	4	3	4	4	4	3	5	3	5	4	5	72
	T61	Round 4	4	4	4	4	5	4	5	4	4	4	6	3	3	6	3	4	6	4	77 -**290**
Graeme McDowell	1	Round 1	4	4	4	4	4	3	3	4	2	4	3	4	3	4	3	4	4	5	66
N Ireland	T9	Round 2	5	4	4	4	5	3	4	4	3	4	4	4	3	4	3	5	4	6	73
£9,950	T25	Round 3	4	4	4	4	5	4	5	4	3	3	3	4	3	5	4	5	4	4	72
	T61	Round 4	5	4	5	4	6	3	4	5	3	5	5	5	3	6	4	5	3	4	79 -**290**
Marco Ruiz	T50	Round 1	4	4	4	4	4	3	4	4	3	4	4	5	3	4	3	4	5	5	71
Paraguay	T37	Round 2	3	4	3	4	4	2	3	4	4	4	4	5	3	4	4	5	4	6	70
£9,750	T70	Round 3	3	6	4	4	5	4	4	4	3	5	4	5	6	5	3	6	4	5	80
	T63	Round 4	5	4	5	3	6	3	3	3	3	4	4	5	3	4	2	4	4	5	70 -**291**
Mark O'Meara	T50	Round 1	4	4	4	5	4	3	4	3	3	4	4	5	3	3	3	5	4	6	71
USA	T37	Round 2	4	5	4	3	5	3	5	4	3	4	3	4	3	4	2	5	5	4	70
£9,750	T64	Round 3	5	4	4	5	5	3	5	4	3	5	3	5	4	4	4	4	4	6	77
	T63	Round 4	4	5	4	4	5	4	4	4	3	4	4	4	3	4	3	5	4	5	73 -**291**
Chad Campbell	T33	Round 1	4	4	4	4	4	3	4	4	4	4	4	5	2	4	3	5	4	4	70
USA	T57	Round 2	5	4	4	4	7	4	4	3	3	5	4	3	3	4	3	5	4	4	73
£9,600	T58	Round 3	4	4	4	3	4	3	4	4	2	5	4	8	3	5	3	5	4	5	74
	65	Round 4	4	4	4	4	5	3	5	4	3	5	4	4	4	5	3	4	5	5	75 -**292**
Vaughn Taylor	T68	Round 1	5	3	3	5	4	4	5	4	4	4	4	4	3	5	3	4	3	5	72
USA	T57	Round 2	5	4	4	4	5	3	4	4	3	5	3	4	2	5	3	5	4	4	71
£9,450	T67	Round 3	4	5	6	4	4	3	6	4	3	5	4	4	4	4	4	5	4	4	77
	T66	Round 4	4	4	4	4	3	3	4	8	3	5	4	4	3	4	3	4	4	6	74 -**294**
Fred Funk	T20	Round 1	4	4	4	6	5	3	3	3	4	4	4	5	2	4	3	4	4	3	69
USA	T57	Round 2	7	5	4	4	4	3	4	4	3	5	4	6	3	4	2	4	4	4	74
£9,450	T64	Round 3	4	4	4	4	5	5	5	4	3	5	4	5	3	4	3	4	4	5	75
	T66	Round 4	5	4	5	5	6	4	5	3	4	5	4	4	3	4	2	4	4	5	76 -**294**
***Edoardo Molinari**	T92	Round 1	3	4	4	4	5	3	5	6	4	4	4	4	2	5	3	3	5	5	73
Italy	T57	Round 2	4	4	5	4	4	3	5	4	3	5	3	5	3	4	2	4	3	5	70
	T67	Round 3	4	4	4	4	5	5	4	4	3	5	4	4	3	5	3	5	6	5	77
	T68	Round 4	4	5	4	4	5	3	5	4	3	4	4	4	4	5	3	5	4	5	75 -**295**

HOLE			1	2	3	4	5	6	7	8	9	10	11	12	13	14	15	16	17	18	
PAR	POSITION		4	4	4	4	5	3	4	4	3	5	4	4	3	4	3	5	4	5	TOTAL
Todd Hamilton	T68	Round 1	4	4	4	4	5	3	3	4	3	4	4	5	3	3	5	5	4	5	72
USA	T57	Round 2	4	4	4	5	4	3	4	4	4	5	4	4	3	4	3	3	4	5	71
£9,300	T58	Round 3	4	4	5	4	5	3	4	4	3	5	4	4	3	4	3	4	5	6	74
	T68	Round 4	4	4	4	4	4	3	4	5	4	5	5	4	3	3	4	6	5	7	78 **-295**
Bart Bryant	T20	Round 1	4	5	4	4	4	3	4	4	2	4	4	4	3	4	3	5	4	4	69
USA	T57	Round 2	6	4	4	4	4	3	4	4	3	5	4	5	3	5	2	4	5	5	74
£9,200	T67	Round 3	5	4	4	4	5	4	4	4	4	5	4	4	3	4	3	4	5	7	77
	70	Round 4	5	5	4	4	6	5	5	4	4	4	4	4	3	4	2	5	4	4	76 **-296**
Paul Casey	T68	Round 1	3	4	5	4	5	3	5	4	4	4	4	4	2	4	4	4	5	4	72
England	T48	Round 2	3	5	4	3	4	3	4	4	2	7	4	4	5	4	2	4	4	4	70
£9,100	T70	Round 3	5	5	4	4	4	3	5	4	2	8	4	4	3	7	3	5	4	5	79
	71	Round 4	6	3	5	4	6	3	5	5	3	5	6	4	3	4	2	4	4	5	77 **-298**

NON QUALIFIERS AFTER 36 HOLES

(Leading 10 professionals and ties receive £3,000 each, next 20 professionals and ties receive £2,500 each, next 20 professionals and ties receive £2,250 each, remainder of professionals receive £2,000 each.)

HOLE			1	2	3	4	5	6	7	8	9	10	11	12	13	14	15	16	17	18	
PAR	POSITION		4	4	4	4	5	3	4	4	3	5	4	4	3	4	3	5	4	5	TOTAL
Rich Beem	T50	Round 1	4	4	4	4	5	3	4	3	3	4	5	5	3	4	4	4	4	4	71
USA	**T72**	Round 2	6	5	4	4	5	3	4	4	3	4	5	4	3	4	3	4	4	4	73 **-144**
Scott Drummond	T92	Round 1	6	4	4	3	5	3	4	3	4	4	4	5	4	4	3	4	4	5	73
Scotland	**T72**	Round 2	5	4	4	5	5	3	4	4	3	4	4	4	3	4	3	4	4	4	71 **-144**
Jeff Maggert	T124	Round 1	5	4	4	4	5	4	3	4	2	4	5	4	4	4	3	4	4	8	75
USA	**T72**	Round 2	5	4	4	4	4	3	4	4	3	3	3	4	3	4	2	4	5	6	69 **-144**
Jarrod Lyle	T108	Round 1	4	4	4	4	5	3	5	4	3	4	4	5	3	6	2	6	4	4	74
Australia	**T72**	Round 2	4	4	4	4	4	3	3	5	3	4	4	3	3	4	3	5	4	6	70 **-144**
Mathew Goggin	T124	Round 1	5	4	4	6	4	3	4	4	3	5	4	5	3	5	4	4	4	4	75
Australia	**T72**	Round 2	4	4	5	5	4	4	4	4	3	4	3	4	3	4	2	5	4	3	69 **-144**
Paul McGinley	T50	Round 1	4	4	4	3	3	4	4	4	4	4	4	4	3	5	3	5	5	4	71
Ireland	**T72**	Round 2	4	4	4	4	6	3	4	5	4	4	3	5	3	4	3	5	4	4	73 **-144**
Markus Brier	T50	Round 1	4	4	4	4	6	4	4	4	3	4	5	4	3	4	3	4	3	4	71
Austria	**T72**	Round 2	4	4	6	4	4	4	4	4	3	5	4	4	3	4	3	5	3	5	73 **-144**
Bradley Dredge	T33	Round 1	5	4	5	4	3	3	4	4	4	4	3	6	3	4	3	4	3	4	70
Wales	**T72**	Round 2	4	5	5	4	3	3	5	4	3	4	5	5	3	5	3	4	4	5	74 **-144**
Niclas Fasth	T20	Round 1	4	4	4	4	5	3	4	4	2	4	4	4	3	5	3	4	4	4	69
Sweden	**T72**	Round 2	5	5	4	3	4	5	4	4	4	5	4	4	3	6	3	4	4	4	75 **-144**
Phillip Price	T108	Round 1	5	4	5	4	6	4	4	3	3	4	5	4	3	4	3	4	4	5	74
Wales	**T72**	Round 2	5	4	4	4	5	3	4	4	3	5	4	4	3	4	2	4	3	5	70 **-144**
Tom Pernice	T50	Round 1	5	3	4	4	5	3	3	4	3	6	4	5	2	4	3	4	4	5	71
USA	**T72**	Round 2	4	4	4	5	5	3	5	4	2	5	5	4	3	4	4	4	4	4	73 **-144**
Mark Pilkington	T137	Round 1	4	4	5	4	4	3	6	4	3	5	4	4	6	4	3	4	4	5	76
Wales	**T72**	Round 2	3	5	3	4	4	3	5	4	3	4	4	4	4	4	2	4	4	4	68 **-144**
Ted Purdy	T108	Round 1	4	5	4	3	5	4	3	6	2	4	4	4	3	4	4	5	5	5	74
USA	**T84**	Round 2	4	4	4	4	5	3	3	5	3	6	3	4	3	5	2	4	4	5	71 **-145**

HOLE			1	2	3	4	5	6	7	8	9	10	11	12	13	14	15	16	17	18	
PAR	POSITION		4	4	4	4	5	3	4	4	3	5	4	4	3	4	3	5	4	5	TOTAL
Lucas Glover	T68	Round 1	6	4	3	4	4	4	4	4	3	4	4	3	4	3	5	4	4	5	72
USA	**T84**	Round 2	4	4	4	4	5	3	3	4	3	4	5	6	3	5	2	4	5	5	73-145
Steve Elkington	T50	Round 1	4	4	4	4	5	3	3	4	3	5	4	5	3	4	3	4	4	5	71
Australia	**T84**	Round 2	4	3	3	6	5	3	4	4	3	4	4	7	3	4	3	6	4	4	74-145
John Daly	T68	Round 1	4	3	4	4	5	3	4	4	3	4	4	5	4	4	3	5	4	5	72
USA	**T84**	Round 2	4	5	5	3	4	3	4	3	3	4	4	4	3	5	4	3	4	8	73-145
Nick O'Hern	T33	Round 1	4	5	4	4	4	4	5	4	3	4	3	4	3	4	3	4	4	4	70
Australia	**T84**	Round 2	5	5	4	4	5	3	5	4	3	4	4	4	3	7	3	4	4	4	75-145
Tom Lehman	T7	Round 1	4	4	4	3	5	3	3	4	3	4	4	4	3	4	3	5	4	4	68
USA	**T84**	Round 2	4	5	4	4	4	3	7	4	3	4	5	4	3	5	3	5	4	6	77-145
Shiv Kapur	T68	Round 1	4	4	4	4	5	3	4	4	3	6	4	4	3	4	3	4	5	4	72
India	**T84**	Round 2	4	4	4	4	5	4	4	4	4	4	4	4	3	5	4	4	4	4	73-145
Sandy Lyle	T92	Round 1	4	5	5	4	4	3	4	4	2	4	4	3	4	5	4	5	4	5	73
Scotland	**T91**	Round 2	4	4	4	4	5	3	5	4	3	4	3	4	4	3	3	5	6	5	73-146
J J Henry	T92	Round 1	4	4	4	4	5	3	3	4	3	4	5	5	4	4	3	4	5	5	73
USA	**T91**	Round 2	4	3	5	4	5	3	5	4	4	4	3	5	3	4	3	5	5	4	73-146
Richard Green	T50	Round 1	3	5	5	4	4	3	5	3	3	5	4	4	3	4	3	4	4	5	71
Australia	**T91**	Round 2	4	5	4	4	5	4	4	4	3	6	4	4	3	5	3	4	4	5	75-146
Aaron Baddeley	T33	Round 1	3	4	4	4	3	3	4	4	3	5	4	4	3	4	4	4	5	4	70
Australia	**T91**	Round 2	5	4	7	3	5	3	4	5	4	5	4	5	3	4	2	5	4	4	76-146
Brett Wetterich	T108	Round 1	4	5	4	4	4	3	5	4	3	5	5	5	4	3	3	5	4	4	74
USA	**T91**	Round 2	4	4	3	4	5	3	5	3	3	4	4	5	3	4	3	5	4	5	72-146
Bo Van Pelt	T108	Round 1	4	6	4	4	4	3	4	4	2	5	4	5	4	5	3	4	5	4	74
USA	**T91**	Round 2	5	4	4	4	4	3	4	4	2	4	4	4	3	4	3	5	7	4	72-146
David Smail	T137	Round 1	5	5	4	3	4	3	4	4	4	5	5	5	3	5	3	5	5	5	76
New Zealand	**T91**	Round 2	4	4	4	4	4	3	4	4	3	4	4	5	3	5	3	4	4	4	70-146
Ben Curtis	T92	Round 1	4	4	4	5	5	3	3	4	3	5	5	5	3	4	3	5	4	4	73
USA	**T91**	Round 2	5	4	5	4	4	3	5	5	3	4	4	4	3	4	2	4	4	6	73-146
K J Choi	T68	Round 1	5	4	5	4	4	4	4	4	4	4	4	4	2	4	3	5	3	6	72
Korea	**T91**	Round 2	4	4	5	5	5	3	5	4	3	4	4	4	3	3	4	5	4	5	74-146
Fred Couples	T33	Round 1	4	5	3	4	5	3	4	4	3	4	4	4	3	4	3	5	4	4	70
USA	**T91**	Round 2	4	5	5	4	6	4	4	4	3	4	5	4	3	4	2	6	5	4	76-146
Vijay Singh	T33	Round 1	4	3	4	5	5	3	4	4	4	4	4	4	3	4	3	4	3	5	70
Fiji	**T91**	Round 2	5	6	4	4	4	4	4	4	3	5	3	4	4	6	3	4	5	4	76-146
Zach Johnson	T92	Round 1	4	4	4	4	4	3	4	4	3	5	5	5	3	4	2	6	5	4	73
USA	**T91**	Round 2	5	5	4	6	6	2	4	4	3	5	3	3	3	4	3	5	4	4	73-146
Stephen Dodd	T92	Round 1	4	6	4	3	5	3	5	4	4	4	4	4	3	3	3	5	4	5	73
Wales	**T91**	Round 2	4	4	4	4	4	2	4	5	3	5	5	5	3	4	3	4	5	5	73-146
Stuart Appleby	T108	Round 1	5	3	5	4	4	3	4	4	3	5	4	4	4	5	3	4	5	5	74
Australia	**T91**	Round 2	4	4	5	4	4	3	4	4	4	4	4	4	4	6	3	4	3	4	72-146
Thomas Aiken	T68	Round 1	4	4	4	4	3	3	6	4	3	4	4	5	4	5	2	4	4	5	72
South Africa	**T91**	Round 2	4	4	5	4	4	3	5	4	3	5	4	4	3	5	3	5	4	5	74-146
Nick Dougherty	T108	Round 1	4	4	4	4	6	4	4	4	3	7	4	4	3	4	3	4	4	4	74
England	**T106**	Round 2	5	5	4	4	6	3	4	4	4	4	3	4	4	4	3	4	4	4	73-147
***Julien Guerrier**	T68	Round 1	4	5	4	4	5	3	4	4	3	4	4	4	4	4	3	4	4	5	72
France	**T106**	Round 2	4	5	4	4	4	3	4	4	2	5	4	5	3	4	3	5	5	7	75-147

HOLE			1	2	3	4	5	6	7	8	9	10	11	12	13	14	15	16	17	18	
PAR	POSITION		4	4	4	4	5	3	4	4	3	5	4	4	3	4	3	5	4	5	TOTAL
Davis Love III	T124	Round 1	4	5	4	4	6	3	4	4	3	4	4	4	4	5	4	4	5	4	75
USA	**T106**	Round 2	4	4	4	4	5	4	4	4	3	5	4	4	3	4	3	5	4	4	72 -147
Louis Oosthuizen	T147	Round 1	4	3	5	4	5	3	4	5	2	7	4	7	4	5	3	4	4	5	78
South Africa	**T106**	Round 2	4	4	4	4	4	3	5	4	3	3	4	4	4	4	3	4	4	4	69 -147
Bradley Hughes	T68	Round 1	5	4	4	5	4	2	4	4	4	5	4	4	3	5	3	4	3	5	72
Australia	**T106**	Round 2	4	4	4	4	5	4	4	4	3	4	4	5	4	5	4	4	4	5	75 -147
Darren Parris	T124	Round 1	5	4	5	4	4	4	4	4	2	5	4	5	4	4	3	6	4	4	75
England	**T106**	Round 2	4	5	5	4	4	3	4	4	4	4	4	3	4	5	3	4	4	4	72 -147
Billy Andrade	T68	Round 1	3	5	4	5	5	3	4	4	3	4	4	6	3	4	3	4	4	4	72
USA	**T106**	Round 2	5	5	4	4	4	5	5	4	2	5	5	5	3	4	3	5	3	4	75 -147
Kenny Perry	T92	Round 1	6	5	5	4	4	3	4	4	3	4	4	4	3	5	3	3	5	4	73
USA	**T106**	Round 2	5	4	5	3	5	3	4	5	3	5	4	5	3	4	3	4	4	5	74 -147
Shaun Micheel	T68	Round 1	5	3	4	4	4	3	4	4	3	5	4	4	3	5	3	5	5	4	72
USA	**T106**	Round 2	4	5	3	5	5	3	4	4	3	5	4	4	3	4	3	5	5	6	75 -147
Michael Wright	T68	Round 1	4	3	4	4	5	3	3	5	2	5	5	4	3	5	3	4	5	5	72
Australia	**T106**	Round 2	4	4	3	5	4	3	6	4	3	5	4	5	4	4	3	5	4	5	75 -147
Adam Bland	T92	Round 1	5	5	4	3	5	3	5	3	3	4	4	4	4	5	2	5	4	5	73
Australia	**T106**	Round 2	4	5	4	4	5	3	4	4	3	4	6	4	4	5	3	5	4	3	74 -147
Shingo Katayama	T108	Round 1	4	5	4	4	4	4	5	4	3	4	4	6	3	4	3	4	4	5	74
Japan	**T117**	Round 2	4	3	4	4	7	4	4	4	3	4	4	4	4	4	3	5	4	5	74 -148
Nick Faldo	T146	Round 1	4	6	4	4	6	4	4	5	3	5	4	4	3	4	2	4	6	5	77
England	**T117**	Round 2	3	3	4	3	5	4	4	5	3	5	5	4	2	4	3	4	4	6	71 -148
Ross Wellington	T124	Round 1	4	5	4	4	4	5	3	4	3	4	4	5	3	5	4	5	5	3	75
South Africa	**T117**	Round 2	4	3	4	4	5	3	4	4	3	4	5	5	2	4	3	6	5	5	73 -148
Bernhard Langer	T108	Round 1	4	5	4	4	4	3	5	6	3	4	4	5	3	4	4	3	5	4	74
Germany	**T117**	Round 2	5	4	4	5	4	3	4	4	3	5	4	5	3	4	4	4	4	5	74 -148
Colin Montgomerie	T92	Round 1	3	4	4	5	5	3	5	4	3	4	4	5	4	4	2	5	4	5	73
Scotland	**T117**	Round 2	5	4	4	4	4	3	4	3	3	4	4	4	4	5	5	6	4	5	75 -148
Arron Oberholser	T92	Round 1	5	4	5	4	4	3	4	4	3	4	3	5	4	5	2	4	5	5	73
USA	**T117**	Round 2	4	5	4	4	5	5	5	4	3	5	4	5	3	4	3	4	4	4	75 -148
Stewart Cink	T68	Round 1	3	4	4	4	4	3	4	7	3	4	4	5	3	4	3	3	4	6	72
USA	**T123**	Round 2	5	5	5	4	4	4	4	4	4	4	4	5	3	5	3	5	4	5	77 -149
Johan Edfors	T124	Round 1	4	5	6	3	4	5	5	4	3	5	3	4	3	5	3	4	5	4	75
Sweden	**T123**	Round 2	4	3	5	4	7	4	4	4	2	6	3	5	3	4	3	4	4	5	74 -149
Richard Sterne	T137	Round 1	4	4	4	4	4	3	5	5	4	5	3	5	3	5	3	6	4	5	76
South Africa	**T123**	Round 2	4	5	5	4	4	3	5	3	3	5	5	5	3	4	1	5	4	5	73 -149
Tim Herron	T137	Round 1	4	5	4	4	5	3	5	4	6	5	4	5	3	4	2	4	4	5	76
USA	**T123**	Round 2	4	4	5	4	3	3	4	4	3	4	5	4	3	6	3	5	4	5	73 -149
Padraig Harrington	T124	Round 1	6	4	4	4	4	3	5	4	3	5	3	4	4	4	3	5	4	6	75
Ireland	**T123**	Round 2	4	5	3	4	6	3	5	3	3	4	4	6	4	4	3	4	5	4	74 -149
Toshinori Muto	T124	Round 1	4	4	4	4	4	3	5	4	3	7	4	4	3	6	2	4	5	5	75
Japan	**T123**	Round 2	4	4	4	4	4	3	6	4	3	4	5	4	3	4	3	5	4	6	74 -149
J B Holmes	T108	Round 1	4	4	5	3	5	4	4	4	4	5	4	4	2	4	3	4	6	5	74
USA	**T123**	Round 2	4	4	4	4	4	5	6	3	3	5	5	4	3	4	3	4	5	5	75 -149
Jim Payne	T92	Round 1	5	4	4	4	4	3	3	4	4	5	3	5	4	4	3	5	4	5	73
England	**T123**	Round 2	5	5	4	5	5	4	5	4	3	6	4	4	3	4	3	4	4	4	76 -149

HOLE			1	2	3	4	5	6	7	8	9	10	11	12	13	14	15	16	17	18	TOTAL
PAR	POSITION		4	4	4	4	5	3	4	4	3	4	4	5	3	4	3	5	4	5	TOTAL
Peter Hedblom	T92	Round 1	4	5	4	4	5	3	4	4	3	4	4	5	3	4	3	5	4	5	73
Sweden	**T131**	Round 2	5	4	4	5	4	4	5	4	4	5	4	5	3	6	3	4	4	4	77 -150
Barry Lane	T124	Round 1	5	4	4	4	5	3	5	4	3	5	6	5	3	3	3	3	4	6	75
England	**T131**	Round 2	4	4	4	5	6	3	4	4	3	5	4	4	3	4	3	6	4	5	75 -150
David Howell	T108	Round 1	4	5	3	4	4	3	4	4	3	6	4	5	3	4	3	4	4	7	74
England	**T131**	Round 2	4	5	3	5	5	3	4	4	3	4	4	6	4	4	3	5	5	5	76 -150
Paul Lawrie	T137	Round 1	4	6	4	5	5	3	4	5	2	4	4	4	3	4	3	6	5	5	76
Scotland	**T131**	Round 2	4	7	5	4	5	2	3	4	3	6	4	5	3	3	4	4	4	4	74 -150
Brett Quigley	151	Round 1	4	4	4	5	5	3	4	4	3	6	5	5	4	5	4	5	4	5	79
USA	**T131**	Round 2	4	3	4	4	4	3	4	4	5	4	4	4	3	5	3	4	4	5	71 -150
Jaime Donaldson	T124	Round 1	4	4	7	3	4	3	6	4	3	5	4	4	3	5	3	4	4	5	75
Wales	**T136**	Round 2	3	4	4	4	4	3	6	4	4	5	4	5	3	6	3	5	4	5	76 -151
Darren Clarke	T20	Round 1	3	4	5	4	5	3	5	4	3	4	3	4	3	4	2	4	4	5	69
N. Ireland	**T136**	Round 2	5	6	4	4	6	3	5	4	3	5	4	5	5	4	4	5	5	5	82 -151
Yasuharu Imano	T92	Round 1	4	5	4	4	5	3	5	4	4	4	4	5	2	4	3	4	4	5	73
Japan	**T136**	Round 2	4	4	5	4	4	3	5	4	4	5	4	4	5	4	3	6	5	5	78 -151
Ian Poulter	T124	Round 1	4	5	4	4	4	3	4	4	2	4	4	4	7	3	5	5	5	5	75
England	**T136**	Round 2	4	5	4	5	5	3	5	4	3	5	5	4	4	4	4	4	4	4	76 -151
Seve Ballesteros	T108	Round 1	5	4	4	4	5	3	5	4	2	4	4	5	4	4	3	5	4	5	74
Spain	**T136**	Round 2	4	5	4	5	4	3	4	5	5	5	5	4	4	2	4	5	4	5	77 -151
Nick Ludwell	T124	Round 1	3	5	5	4	5	3	4	4	3	4	4	3	3	7	3	5	5	5	75
England	**T136**	Round 2	4	4	4	4	5	3	4	4	3	4	4	3	3	5	5	3	6	8	76 -151
Bruce Vaughan	T124	Round 1	4	4	4	5	6	4	4	4	4	5	5	4	3	6	3	3	3	4	75
USA	**T142**	Round 2	6	5	7	4	5	4	4	4	3	4	4	4	3	4	3	4	5	4	77 -152
Tatsuhiko Ichihara	T147	Round 1	5	4	5	5	4	3	4	4	4	5	6	4	6	2	3	5	4	5	78
Japan	**T142**	Round 2	4	5	4	4	5	2	4	5	3	5	4	4	4	3	5	4	4	5	74 -152
Warren Bladon	T137	Round 1	3	5	5	4	5	5	5	4	3	4	4	3	4	3	4	4	4	7	76
England	**T142**	Round 2	4	5	5	5	3	4	5	3	5	4	6	2	4	3	5	4	4	5	76 -152
Adam Frayne	T50	Round 1	4	4	3	4	5	3	6	4	3	5	3	4	2	5	3	3	5	5	71
England	**T142**	Round 2	4	4	6	4	5	3	4	4	3	5	5	4	3	6	3	6	4	8	81 -152
Warren Abery	T137	Round 1	5	5	4	5	4	5	5	4	2	5	3	5	3	4	3	4	4	6	76
South Africa	**146**	Round 2	5	4	4	5	4	3	5	4	4	5	5	5	4	4	3	5	4	4	77 -153
*Danny Denison	T147	Round 1	4	5	6	5	5	3	5	4	4	6	4	5	3	4	3	4	4	4	78
England	**T147**	Round 2	4	4	5	4	5	3	5	4	3	5	4	4	4	5	4	4	4	5	76 -154
Gary Lockerbie	T147	Round 1	5	4	5	4	5	3	6	5	3	4	4	6	3	4	3	5	4	4	78
England	**T147**	Round 2	5	5	5	4	5	3	5	4	3	5	4	3	6	3	4	3	4	5	76 -154
Wayne Perske	T137	Round 1	4	5	3	4	5	3	4	5	3	4	5	4	4	3	4	4	4	7	76
Australia	**149**	Round 2	5	4	9	3	5	3	4	4	2	7	5	4	4	5	3	4	4	4	79 -155
Unho Park	T153	Round 1	4	5	5	5	7	3	3	5	4	4	4	4	4	5	4	6	5	5	82
Australia	**150**	Round 2	6	4	4	4	4	4	5	4	3	4	5	5	3	4	3	4	4	4	74 -156
Carlos Rodiles	152	Round 1	5	4	5	4	6	4	4	5	3	4	5	4	3	5	4	5	5	4	81
Spain	**T151**	Round 2	5	4	4	5	4	4	4	4	3	5	4	5	2	5	3	5	5	5	76 -157
Sam Little	156	Round 1	6	5	5	4	5	4	5	5	3	5	4	5	3	6	4	5	5	4	83
England	**T151**	Round 2	5	5	6	4	5	4	4	4	3	4	3	4	3	4	3	4	4	5	74 -157
Ben Bunny	T108	Round 1	4	5	4	4	5	3	4	4	3	5	4	5	3	4	3	5	5	4	74
Australia	**T151**	Round 2	4	5	7	5	4	4	8	4	3	5	4	4	3	5	3	6	5	4	83 -157

HOLE		1	2	3	4	5	6	7	8	9	10	11	12	13	14	15	16	17	18	
PAR	POSITION	4	4	4	4	5	3	4	4	3	5	4	4	3	4	3	5	4	5	TOTAL
Gary Day	T153	Round 1	4	7	5	4	5	4	5	4	5	6	4	4	4	4	3	4	4	6	82
England	**154**	Round 2	5	4	5	4	5	4	4	3	3	5	5	4	3	6	3	4	4	5	76 -158
Jon Bevan	T153	Round 1	6	5	5	5	5	4	6	5	5	5	4	4	2	4	3	5	5	4	82
England	**155**	Round 2	5	5	4	3	5	3	4	5	4	4	5	4	5	5	3	6	5	6	81 -163
Kenneth Ferrie	T137	Round 1	4	5	4	4	4	4	4	4	3	7	5	5	3	4	2	4	4	6	76
England	**156**	Round 2	4	5	4	4	6	3	4												WD

THE TOP TENS Courtesy of Unisys

Birdies

1. **Chris DiMarco** 25
2. Hideto Tanihara 24
3. Jim Furyk 21
4. Adam Scott 20
4. Ernie Els 20
6. *Tiger Woods* *19*
6. Carl Pettersson 19
6. Peter Lonard 19
6. Mike Weir 19
6. Mark Hensby 19
6. Angel Cabrera 19

Pars

1. **Michael Campbell** 51
2. Chad Campbell 50
2. Todd Hamilton 50
4. Rod Pampling 49
5. Lee Slattery 48
6. Geoff Ogilvy 47
6. Sergio Garcia 47
6. S K Ho 47
6. Ben Crane 47
6. Thomas Bjorn 47
6. Anthony Wall 47
6. Stephen Ames 47
6. *Edoardo Molinari 47
38. Tiger Woods 43

Bogeys

1. **Carlos Rodiles** 16
1. **Brett Rumford** 16
3. Mark O'Meara 15
3. Soren Kjeldsen 15
3. Mark Hensby 15
3. Jon Bevan 15
7. Brandt Jobe 14
7. Simon Khan 14
7. Miguel Angel Jimenez 14
7. Marco Ruiz 14
7. Retief Goosen 14
7. Unho Park 14
68. Tiger Woods 7

Double Bogeys/Worse

1. **Paul Casey** 4/2
2. Jon Bevan 4/0
2. Mike Weir 4/0
4. Fred Funk 3/1
4. Adam Frayne 3/1
4. Jamie Donaldson 3/1
7. 11 players tied 3/0
51. Tiger Woods 0/0

Driving Distance

1. **Andrew Buckle** 320.8
2. Robert Karlsson 314.0
3. Andres Romero 313.4
4. Retief Goosen 311.4
5. Angel Cabrera 310.6
6. Adam Scott 309.5
7. Ben Crane 309.0
8. Robert Rock 308.8
9. G Fernandez-Castano .. 308.4
10. Phil Mickelson 308.0
53. Tiger Woods 290.9

Fairways Hit

Maximum of 54

1. *Tiger Woods* *48*
2. Mark Calcavecchia 46
3. Greg Owen 45
3. Scott Verplank 45
5. Fred Funk 44
6. Keiichiro Fukabori 43
6. Chad Campbell 43
6. Carl Pettersson 43
6. *Marius Thorp 43
6. Lee Westwood 43

Greens in Regulation

Maximum of 72

1. **Michael Campbell** 59
2. *Tiger Woods* *58*
2. Chad Campbell 58
2. Greg Owen 58
5. Andres Romero 56
5. Ernie Els 56
7. Andrew Buckle 55
7. Chris DiMarco 55
7. Carl Pettersson 55
7. Robert Rock 55
7. Robert Allenby 55
7. Angel Cabrera..................55

Putts

1. **Brett Rumford** 109
2. Simon Dyson 110
3. Chris DiMarco 112
3. Mikko Ilonen 112
5. Jim Furyk 113
5. S K Ho 113
7. Thaworn Wiratchant 114
8. Marco Ruiz 115
8. Geoff Ogilvy 115
10. Hideto Tanihara 116
10. Fred Funk 116
31. Tiger Woods 120

Statistical Rankings
Courtesy of Unisys

	Driving Distance	Rank	Fairways Hit	Rank	Greens In Regulation	Rank	Putts	Rank
Robert Allenby	301.1	21	42	11	55	7	120	31
Stephen Ames	300.3	25	34	59	48	41	117	12
John Bickerton	272.3	70	39	31	52	23	125	55
Thomas Bjorn	299.9	28	37	37	47	50	121	38
Paul Broadhurst	300.5	24	33	66	48	41	120	31
Bart Bryant	290.1	55	37	37	49	37	130	66
Andrew Buckle	320.8	1	38	35	55	7	130	66
Angel Cabrera	310.6	5	34	59	55	7	121	38
Mark Calcavecchia	282.8	64	46	2	53	18	126	59
Chad Campbell	297.6	34	43	6	58	2	134	71
Michael Campbell	299.6	30	40	23	59	1	131	68
Paul Casey	305.4	16	35	51	51	27	129	65
Tim Clark	288.1	58	36	43	45	61	119	23
Ben Crane	309.0	7	35	51	54	13	122	45
Chris DiMarco	279.6	67	42	11	55	7	112	3
Luke Donald	295.8	40	35	51	46	55	118	17
David Duval	300.6	23	36	43	45	61	118	17
Simon Dyson	305.4	16	39	31	42	69	110	2
Ernie Els	295.4	44	40	23	56	5	118	17
G Fernandez-Castano	308.4	9	27	70	47	50	119	23
Marcus Fraser	275.1	69	42	11	47	50	119	23
Keiichiro Fukabori	298.0	32	43	6	50	33	125	55
Fred Funk	286.6	62	44	5	43	68	116	10
Jim Furyk	291.6	52	42	11	48	41	113	5
Sergio Garcia	306.3	13	42	11	52	23	117	12
Retief Goosen	311.4	4	36	43	50	33	121	38
Todd Hamilton	291.8	51	37	37	44	64	123	50
Mark Hensby	297.1	35	36	43	46	55	118	17
S K Ho	284.6	63	39	31	46	55	113	5
Mikko Ilonen	299.8	29	35	51	46	55	112	3
Miguel Angel Jimenez	292.6	48	31	68	46	55	119	23
Brandt Jobe	305.8	15	34	59	49	37	125	55
Robert Karlsson	314.0	2	40	23	48	41	123	50
Jerry Kelly	279.5	68	42	11	53	18	122	45
Simon Khan	295.8	40	40	23	49	37	119	23
Soren Kjeldsen	281.9	65	41	20	44	64	119	23
Peter Lonard	297.9	33	34	59	51	27	118	17
Hunter Mahan	307.5	11	39	31	54	13	128	62
Andrew Marshall	270.0	71	42	11	46	55	121	38
Graeme McDowell	295.5	42	40	23	53	18	133	70
Phil Mickelson	308.0	10	35	51	50	33	121	38
*Edoardo Molinari	293.3	46	32	67	44	64	122	45
Geoff Ogilvy	296.6	37	42	11	48	41	115	8
Sean O'Hair	300.3	25	40	23	53	18	123	50
Jose Maria Olazabal	292.4	50	35	51	47	50	122	45
Mark O'Meara	289.1	57	35	51	50	33	128	62
Greg Owen	307.5	11	45	3	58	2	131	68
Rod Pampling	295.1	45	41	20	54	13	126	59
Carl Pettersson	301.5	20	43	6	55	7	121	38
Robert Rock	308.8	8	23	71	55	7	119	23
Andres Romero	313.4	3	36	43	56	5	120	31
Marco Ruiz	297.1	35	34	59	40	70	115	8
Brett Rumford	292.6	48	37	37	40	70	109	1
Rory Sabbatini	287.5	59	36	43	47	50	117	12
Charl Schwartzel	301.1	21	35	51	51	27	118	17
Adam Scott	309.5	6	34	59	51	27	117	12
John Senden	303.3	18	38	35	54	13	121	38
Lee Slattery	303.1	19	28	69	48	41	117	12
Jeff Sluman	290.6	54	37	37	49	37	120	31
Henrik Stenson	305.9	14	40	23	52	23	123	50
Hideto Tanihara	295.5	42	36	43	53	18	116	10
Vaughn Taylor	300.1	27	40	23	48	41	124	54
*Marius Thorp	298.3	31	43	6	45	61	119	23
Scott Verplank	280.9	66	45	3	54	13	128	62
Simon Wakefield	289.6	56	34	59	48	41	120	31
Anthony Wall	287.3	60	37	37	52	23	120	31
Tom Watson	292.8	47	42	11	48	41	122	45
Mike Weir	295.9	39	41	20	51	27	126	59
Lee Westwood	296.6	37	43	6	51	27	125	55
Thaworn Wiratchant	287.0	61	36	43	44	64	114	7
Tiger Woods	290.9	53	48	1	58	2	120	31

Rank indicates position (including ties) after 72 holes.

NON QUALIFIERS AFTER 36 HOLES

	Driving Distance	Rank	Fairways Hit	Rank	Greens In Regulation	Rank	Putts	Rank
Warren Abery	289.3	91	20	50	19	138	64	119
Thomas Aiken	305.3	20	17	110	21	124	56	13
Billy Andrade	283.5	113	26	1	24	73	65	127
Stuart Appleby	291.0	82	24	3	24	73	63	99
Aaron Baddeley	299.0	40	16	127	26	30	61	62
Severiano Ballesteros	277.0	139	19	74	17	149	60	52
Rich Beem	293.5	68	20	50	26	30	59	40
Jon Bevan	279.0	132	19	74	15	154	64	119
Warren Bladon	286.8	101	14	148	17	149	59	40
Adam Bland	284.0	110	23	12	26	30	65	127
Markus Brier	283.8	111	23	12	31	3	66	141
Ben Bunny	294.0	64	19	74	18	143	63	99
K J Choi	294.0	64	17	110	26	30	65	127
Stewart Cink	310.0	12	17	110	19	138	59	40
Darren Clarke	292.3	74	19	74	19	138	58	24
Fred Couples	278.8	133	15	136	22	110	61	62
Ben Curtis	289.5	88	20	50	24	73	62	82
John Daly	310.0	12	11	155	22	110	61	62
Gary Day	279.5	127	18	90	19	138	66	141
*Danny Denison	269.3	153	23	12	18	143	63	99
Stephen Dodd	275.8	143	17	110	24	73	65	127
Jamie Donaldson	278.8	133	23	12	25	56	62	82
Nick Dougherty	298.5	45	15	136	24	73	62	82
Bradley Dredge	284.5	107	15	136	24	73	60	52
Scott Drummond	285.8	103	21	37	24	73	63	99
Johan Edfors	320.3	4	16	127	21	124	62	82
Steve Elkington	288.8	94	21	37	26	30	61	62
Nick Faldo	283.5	113	22	27	25	56	65	127
Niclas Fasth	302.5	27	18	90	25	56	65	127
Adam Frayne	266.3	155	19	74	25	56	66	141
Lucas Glover	311.5	7	18	90	25	56	64	119
Mathew Goggin	304.3	21	18	90	24	73	64	119
Richard Green	280.3	123	19	74	25	56	63	99
*Julien Guerrier	291.8	76	21	37	26	30	66	141
Padraig Harrington	286.5	102	17	110	21	124	61	62
Peter Heblom	278.0	135	20	50	23	93	66	141
J J Henry	301.3	32	19	74	30	7	69	153
Tim Herron	291.0	82	18	90	23	93	62	82
J B Holmes	326.8	1	19	74	23	93	65	127
David Howell	289.3	91	15	136	20	132	63	99
Bradley Hughes	294.0	64	20	50	23	93	62	82
Tatsuhiko Ichihara	299.0	40	20	50	23	93	67	149
Yasuharu Imano	279.8	125	19	74	22	110	62	82
Zach Johnson	275.5	144	20	50	17	149	55	8
Shiv Kapur	287.0	98	26	1	21	124	58	24
Shingo Katayama	292.5	73	22	27	23	93	61	62
Barry Lane	272.5	149	20	50	25	56	67	149
Bernhard Langer	287.0	98	20	50	22	110	62	82
Paul Lawrie	295.8	57	16	127	22	110	63	99
Tom Lehman	287.5	97	22	27	26	30	61	62
Sam Little	276.5	141	20	50	22	110	66	141
Gary Lockerbie	291.3	78	19	74	22	110	65	127
Davis Love III	310.5	10	22	27	24	73	63	99
Nick Ludwell	275.5	144	17	110	25	56	65	127
Jarrod Lyle	295.5	58	15	136	25	56	60	52
Sandy Lyle	303.3	23	13	150	21	124	60	52
Jeff Maggert	291.3	78	23	12	25	56	63	99
Paul McGinley	291.0	82	23	12	24	73	62	82
Shaun Micheel	300.0	39	21	37	23	93	63	99
Colin Montgomerie	293.0	71	24	3	22	110	64	119
Toshinori Muto	277.8	136	20	50	25	56	65	127
Arron Oberholser	279.5	127	18	90	25	56	62	82
Nick O'Hern	277.5	137	17	110	26	30	62	82
Louis Oosthuizen	300.5	37	15	136	24	73	61	62
Unho Park	287.0	98	17	110	16	152	63	99
Darren Parris	275.3	146	18	90	20	132	58	24
Jim Payne	268.3	154	20	50	20	132	61	62
Tom Pernice	279.5	127	23	12	24	73	59	40
Kenny Perry	299.0	40	17	110	20	132	59	40
Wayne Perske	293.3	70	16	127	18	143	57	15
Mark Pilkington	302.8	26	16	127	18	143	52	2
Ian Poulter	285.3	105	20	50	20	132	61	62
Phillip Price	280.5	121	18	90	23	93	61	62
Ted Purdy	296.3	55	21	37	28	13	67	149
Brett Quigley	302.0	29	15	136	18	143	61	62
Carlos Rodiles	296.8	54	13	150	16	152	62	82
Vijay Singh	298.5	45	19	74	27	22	66	141
David Smail	301.0	34	21	37	24	73	63	99
Richard Sterne	293.5	68	13	150	15	154	51	1
Bo Van Pelt	314.8	6	16	127	26	30	64	119
Bruce Vaughan	285.3	105	15	136	22	110	64	119
Ross Wellington	292.0	75	13	150	18	143	55	8
Brett Wetterich	311.3	8	13	150	23	93	62	82
Michael Wright	283.8	111	15	136	23	93	64	119

Rank indicates position (including ties) after 36 holes.

PHOTOGRAPHY CREDITS

Express Newspapers – 18

Rolex/Chris Turvey – 107 left

(All others © Getty Images)

Scott Barbour – 17

David Cannon – front cover, 8, 9, 10, 12, 21 (Bevan), 21 (Day), 26 top, 33 right, 41, 60, 76 right, 84, 86, 87, 89 bottom, 95, 102-103 bottom

Kristian Dowling – 22 (Wright)

Stuart Franklin –23 (Abery), 35 top right, 36 top, 36 bottom, 47, 48, 49 left, 49 right, 50 left, 50 middle, 52, 58 top right, 58 bottom, 61, 64, 68, 72 (2), 75, 79, 80 top, 81 bottom left, 81 bottom right, 89 top, 91 top right, 93, 102 top, 108 left, 109 middle, 111 right, 112 top left, 113

Scott Halleran – 22 (Pernice)

Richard Heathcote – 23 (Oosthuizen)

Ross Kinnaird – 16, 24, 29 right, 30, 31 bottom left, 32, 40, 42 top, 46, 50 right, 53 bottom, 70 bottom, 74, 90, 91 bottom, 105, 109 left, 111 left

Matthew Lewis – 21 (Payne)

Warren Little – 27, 31 bottom right, 33 left, 34, 42 bottom, 44, 57, 58 top left, 63, 69, 78, 80 bottom, 91 left, 92 top right, 108 middle, 109 right, 114

Andy Lyons – 28, 31 top, 38, 51, 53 top, 54 bottom, 67, 71, 77 top right, 81 top, 82, 83, 88 left, 92 top left, 101, 103 top

Stephen Munday – 14

Andrew Redington – back cover, 6, 21 (Ludwell), 26 bottom, 29 left, 35 top left, 35 bottom, 37, 43, 54 top, 55 (3), 59 (2), 66, 70 top, 73, 76 left, 77 top left, 77 bottom, 88 right, 92 bottom, 94,96, 98, 104, 107 right, 108 right, 110, 112 top right, 112 bottom

Phil Walker – 22 (Lyle)

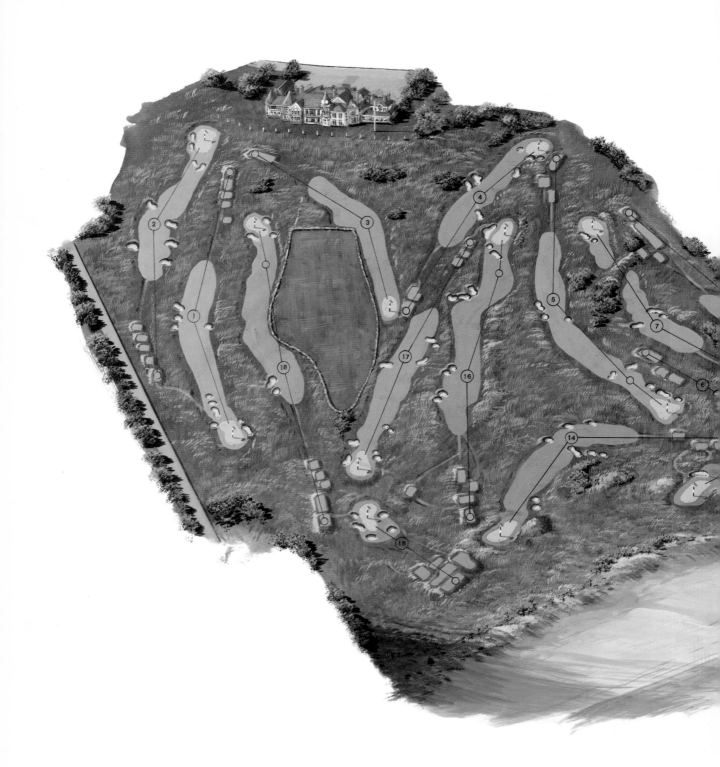